TIME TO ENJOY THE MOMENT

Contents

RISKS, SCRAPES AND STRANGE JOURNEYS

DARING TO DO SOMETHING DIFFERENT

CLOSE ENCOUNTERS WITH LOCAL CULTURES

Foreword: Oldies on the Move
Dervla Murphy

In her late thirties, Jane Austen serenely prepared for imminent middle age and soon was dressing as a maiden aunt with no hope of losing her maidenhood. Yet many of her relatives and friends lived energetically into their eighties and nineties; so why, two hundred years ago, was middle age allowed to take over at forty? Was the bible to blame? Until recently, its general prognosis seemed realistic: threescore years and ten if you were lucky. My own generation took this ration so much for granted that I now feel absurdly smug about being thirteen years into overtime. True, these last few years have revealed several tiresome worn parts, but the underlying logic here – that all machines wear out – makes restricted physical activity seem tolerable. And this despite the fact that the wanderlust, unlike other lusts, does not diminish with age.

For this reason one should avoid, for as long as possible, casual visits to the doctor. He/she is too likely to take blood samples, diagnose problems you haven't yet noticed, prescribe medicines that benefit only Big Pharma and advise you not to go where you want to go.

In 1992, when I decided to cycle from Nairobi to Cape Town, my family and friends made no comment; it was the sort of thing Dervla did. Only a few anxious acquaintances, and sceptical interviewing journalists, drew my attention to the fact that I was aged sixty-one;

it wasn't yet trendy to witter on about 'sixty being forty' and 'eighty being sixty'.

In fact, ever since the bicycle was invented, cyclists have kept pedalling into their old age. Quite often one hears of grannies and granddads cycling across the USA or Canada, or from Helsinki to Gibraltar, or from Mexico to Patagonia. That's the convenient thing about non-competitive cycling (or walking): the more of it you do, on a daily basis, the longer you can keep doing it. Before affluence hit Ireland, many GAA fans from my home town of Lismore thought nothing of cycling over the Knockmealdown mountains, on bicycles without gears, to an important hurling match in Thurles. They set out at sunrise and arrived home in the summer dusk having pedalled 120 miles. Now their grandchildren motor to fetch the milk from a shop around the corner.

Between Nairobi airport and the Zambezi River (a three-month cycle via Kenya, Uganda, Tanzania, Zambia and Malawi) my grey hair and wrinkles worried many of those who offered hospitality. Staying in villages and small towns, I aroused much sympathy. Why was I – an elderly white traveller, and therefore rich – using a poor person's form of transport? Why was an obvious granny so far from home instead of fulfilling her natural role? Was my husband dead? Had I lost all my children to some catastrophe? (I was on the Ukimwi Road, traversing countries newly devastated by AIDS; in too many villages the oldies were rearing orphaned grandchildren.) Total incomprehension greeted my explanation about being a travel writer. South of the Limpopo, where the apartheid era was nearing its end, my whiteness rather than my age drew comment. Whoever heard of a white woman cycling? Never mind pedalling solo all over South Africa's states… However, friends remarked that in a few dodgy areas the grey hair and wrinkles (both accentuated by months of exposure to African sun) probably had a certain amulet effect.

In Siberia, in 2002 and 2004 (summer and winter journeys), being a babushka was a huge bonus. My contemporaries laughed and hugged me and feigned disbelief on being told my age. Their anxious children asked my advice about their struggle to cope with the austerities of post-Soviet life in small towns untouched by the new prosperity of European Russia. Meanwhile the bouncy grandchildren enjoyed playing with this bizarre sort of babushka who spent so much time writing that one six-year-old asked if I'd started school again (which prompted me to recall the term 'second childhood' – so much gentler than 'dementia' or 'Alzheimer's'). Only when dealing with local bureaucrats did I encounter an age problem; they refused to believe that a genuine foreign babushka would go wandering alone in Siberia – especially in mid-winter. I must be something sinister in disguise. A CIA agent? An oil industry commercial spy? Without my new friends' vigorous support, I might never have reached the Pacific coast.

Nowadays, some interviewers ask: 'For travellers, is aging an advantage or a disadvantage?' And of course the answer depends, to some extent, on where and how you want to travel. In Europe, as digital devices oust the fellow-humans who used to sell tickets and give information about times and platform numbers, travelling can become stressful for oldies with failing eyesight, advancing deafness and an allergy to complex, swiftly moving machines which give you no time to fumble with your purse. (I won't go to the nostalgic extreme of recalling men known as 'porters' who carried luggage…) Moreover, even pre-digital Europe had begun to seem indifferent to, if not impatient of, elderly travellers – and though I can think of many helpful exceptions, they are exceptions.

However, in the former 'Third World' one is, on the whole, conscious of being respected (perhaps undeservedly) for one's superior wisdom or at least for having acquired experience of a depth made available only by time. It often occurs to me that being a Western oldie is fine for those who relish solitude; but not much fun for those who live alone, not needed, not valued for their hard-earned wisdom, feeling surplus to requirement. In places where extended families and close-knit communities survive the ravages of globalisation, oldies have a distinct advantage.

I used to secretly pride myself on being adaptable (which included splitting infinitives at my own discretion). But recently a granddaughter observed that I am only adaptable backwards. I can live happily for months far from piped water, electricity, tarred roads, motor transport, radio, telephone, typewriter, post office. These, after all, are non-essentials – novelties, in historical terms – and anyone born in 1931 should be able to adjust to their absence.

At seventy-seven, one can't cycle or walk as many miles per diem as one could at sixty-seven. During my several journeys in Palestine/ Israel I bussed and walked instead of cycling and there being grey, wrinkled, bent and sometimes lame provided immunity in a few situations which might have been awkward for a younger traveller. On my seventy-seventh birthday, I celebrated by walking many miles through an uninhabited and dramatically beautiful corner of the Negev. And while resting beside a weirdly eroded grotto I pondered our absurd reluctance calmly to grow old. Sitting beside a spring-fed pool – once on the Sabaean merchants' camel trail to the port of Gaza – I reflected that there was nothing new about the yearnings to prolong youth or defy death; the ancients had lots to say about drinking from the fountain of eternal youth. And most peoples' mythologies record a variety of death-dodging rituals, songs, relationships, diets and disguises.

In the travellers' world, social media have enlarged the generation gap. The internet has brought a change in the very concept of travel as a process taking one away from the familiar into the unknown. Now the familiar is not left behind and the unknown has become familiar before one leaves home. Unpredictability – to my generation, the salt that gave travelling its savour – seems unnecessary if not downright irritating to many of the young. The sunset challenge – where to sleep? – has been banished by the ease of booking into a hostel or organised campsite with street-plan provided by the internet. Moreover, relatives and friends evidently expect regular reassurance about the traveller's precise location and welfare – and vice versa, the traveller needing to know that all is well back home.

Notoriously, dependence on instant communication with distant family and friends is known to stunt the development of self-reliance. Perhaps this is why, among younger travellers, one notices a new timidity. It worries me to hear youngsters muttering uneasily, 'I don't think we can go there, we can't speak the language.' In pre-web days, serious travellers didn't allow those limits to determine destinations. We knew that on the practical level, sign-language is adequate. If you're hungry, thirsty, sleepy, dirty, sore, needing to pee, needing food for your equine companion – such needs can be conveyed wordlessly. (Even to the point of specifying how to cook your egg; on all continents frying eggs make the same noise.) For ten weeks, in the highlands of Ethiopia in 1967, I met not one English-speaker yet had no language problem. (There were many others!)

As an oldie, one can largely ignore all this – even if it does mean that at travellers' meeting places oldies find themselves oddly isolated while the rest go online instead of communicating, as of yore, with their fellow-travellers. Had Facebook and Twitterings taken over by March 1979, when my daughter and I first met Hilary Bradt in an Andean doss-house, we would have missed out on a lifelong friendship and you might not be reading this foreword.

Introduction
Hilary Bradt

Matthew Parris recently wrote in *The Times*: 'As the years close in the temptation to become dignified becomes so very strong. We must fight it to the last.'

The abandonment of dignity is, in many cases, what this book is about. The stories collected here are by people over sixty who dared to defy stereotypes and test their ageing limbs and minds against physical and mental endeavour. Some are by professional travel writers, others winning entries in a competition we launched in conjunction with Silver Travel Advisor (the website offering travel advice for mature travellers), promoting it through channels including *The Oldie* magazine and the University of the Third Age (U3A). Inspiring stories poured in. A woman celebrated her sixtieth birthday cycling from Calais to Cumbria – via Japan; a man revisited a school in Sierra Leone where he'd taught fifty years ago; and a woman with a fear of heights jumped off a mountain to fly with a vulture. And perhaps the most unusual of all, a cruise passenger approached a prostitute in Saint Petersburg with an unexpected request.

We pensioners know what many youngsters find hard to believe: that our best years are often in our Third Age. This is when we have time and – if we are fortunate – our health to do exactly as we want.

It's our last chance. It's now or never. Carpe diem!

A Physical Challenge

The Hat

Anne Sigmon

Such a ruckus this afternoon, I thought, swirling my dog-tired feet in the hotel pool. My reflection rippled across the surface as I flexed my arches and wiggled my toes in the bathtub-warm water. I felt like a cartoon Madeline in my straw topper with the big upturned brim. Maybe that was it, I thought. Maybe it was all about the hat.

It was our first evening in Thanjavur in South India's Tamil Nadu state. As I fanned myself with the hat, my hair fluttered in the hairdryer breeze, a welcome relief from the blast-furnace heat of midday. This kind of debilitating heat was, my doctor had warned, strictly taboo for me – a stroke and autoimmune patient with water-thin blood.

South India had been my husband's idea. 'You'll love it,' Jack promised. 'We'll be careful. It won't be *that* hot.

Though I wanted to love it, I couldn't shake my reservations.

When Jack thought of South India, he envisioned ninth-century temples, exquisite bronze statuary and enigmatic paintings deep inside ancient caves. My expectations ran to malarial mosquitoes, food-borne illnesses – and the scary side-effects of the drugs I'd have to take to prevent the same; not to mention bird flu, heatstroke and two-lane roads choked with four lanes of bicycle carts bumping into ambling cows, cars dodging auto rickshaws, and circus-painted trucks racing uphill around blind curves to pass beeping buses. There were at least nineteen probable ways I imagined I could die on a trip like this.

'Stop agonising,' Jack said. 'You'll be fine.'

Even nearing seventy, he was fit and fearless. When it came to travel, the more god-forsaken, mosquito-infested, rundown and chaotic the place, the better Jack loved it – just so long as there were temples to climb and caves to crawl through. Thanjavur was his kind of place all right, I thought, soaking my toasted tootsies in the pool.

Pre-Jack, as a middle-aged klutz with a delicate constitution – a wuss, really – my idea of adventure travel ran to out-of-the-way Mexican beaches. Then, nearing forty, I married Jack and, in ignorant love, traipsed along with him to Borneo where we took tea with erstwhile headhunters and I was half-nelsoned by an over-exuberant orangutan. Having survived that – actually, having loved it – there wasn't much left to fear from travel. Over our first decade of marriage, we stalked cougars on horseback in the Canadian Rockies, huffed our way up Mount Kilimanjaro, even once bunked with a tribe of Huli Wigmen in Papua New Guinea where we were protected from a rival tribe by six guys in grass skirts carrying bows and arrows plus one alarmingly homemade shotgun. Indian temples should have seemed tame by comparison. And they would have, too, but for the stroke.

Shortly after Papua New Guinea, I was zapped out of the blue by a stroke I later learned was caused by an obscure (and supremely unpronounceable) autoimmune disease that turns my blood to clot-happy sludge. (The disease is called Antiphospholipid Syndrome – APS for short.) I wasn't yet fifty years old.

On that eerie morning when the stroke hit, I was lost in a mental whiteout, unable to remember my address, my husband's name, or how to dial 911. In the year that followed, I had to relearn the alphabet, how to hold a fork, how to tie my shoes. I had to relearn to type in spite of a therapist who thought my time would be better spent braiding potholders. That year I also had to learn, kicking and screaming, how to be a patient with a serious chronic illness taking a scary-high level of blood thinner to prevent another stroke.

As I started, oh so gingerly, to travel again, my doctors cautioned me sternly to get plenty of rest and take it easy, avoid overheating, dehydration, infection and accidents and, above all, never, ever to hit my head. Adventure travel in my state of health, they seemed to imply, was like a fifteen-year-old with a learner's permit competing in the Indy 500.

But being stubborn, or optimistic – or both – I couldn't give up travelling. I was careful. I watched my medicine, had my blood tested. I weighed the risks. And usually, after some handwringing, I went: to western China, to Burma, Vietnam and Laos. But even after years of post-stroke travel, I still couldn't help worrying. It was like, at sixty, I'd morphed back into the old scaredy-pants me.

This trip, I was giving it my best. That morning, our first at Thanjavur, we headed straight for the temple complex. Jack approached each sanctuary with the excitement of an archaeologist discovering a new site, charging from carving to statue to Sanskrit inscription, clutching his guidebook, inventorying each sculpture and checking it off. He was in his element, counting temple parts – *gopurums, mandapas, antarlas; kutas, shalas, panjaras* – and identifying avatars of Vishnu and incarnations of Shiva.

There wasn't much our poor local guide, Ajit, could do except watch me struggling to keep up, looking like a senior Dora Explorer, my day-bag slung across my chest like a bandolier, my straw hat askew, my camera and water bottle flopping as I teetered tender-footed on the broiling paving stones – no shoes allowed in the temple precinct. Ajit split the difference between us, rushing up to offer a bit of temple lore to Jack, dashing back to extend a hand as I navigated steep granite steps in my slick sock feet.

In between forays into the sun to admire the carvings, I found a tiny half-circle of shade under a palm tree, where I reapplied sunscreen, sipped water spiked with electrolyte mix and watched the parade of pilgrims. There were families mostly, large ones: old men in sweat-soaked tank tops and white dhotis, younger men in slacks and loose cotton shirts or natty polos. The women all wore saris in lush colours and exuberant prints. Grandmas toted picnic satchels and mothers carried babies, their bangle bracelets clicking as they padded nonchalantly over the scorching pavement. Swirling around them was a sea of children, roguish boys in a blur of motion, little girls in stiff organdy dresses, teens in smart *salwar kameez* – tunics over long flowing pants that brought to mind a demure Scheherazade.

Most groups swept through the temple in a half-hour swish of rainbow-coloured saris. More thoughtful visitors stayed for an hour, still not enough for me. Even with the sun and the hot sock feet, I was happily engaged for a good two hours, admiring the exquisite modelling of a goddess's face carved in thousand-year-old sandstone, laughing at the row of elephants dancing upright along the base of the temple – a ten-ton conga line still fresh and whimsical almost a millennium after it was carved. I watched, fascinated, as a troupe of musicians paraded through the courtyard, pounding drums and sounding the high, atonal *nadaswaram* (a horn) to signal the time for *pooja* or worship.

But by hour three in the broiling sun, I was over-hot, overtired and cranky with achy, burning feet, searching desperately for a shady corner inside the temple to plot murder. I batted feebly at the muggy air with a balsawood fan I'd bought from a vendor, one of its blades already broken and taped, to little effect, with my emergency Band-Aid.

Listening from my shady sanctuary, I heard Ajit tell Jack there are more than four hundred major Hindu temples in Tamil Nadu state alone. *Heaven help me, Jack's going to want to see them all*, I thought, slouching into my corner. Leaning against the cool interior stone, I took a long last drink of water, then drained the bottle onto my bandana to wet my face, always tomato-red in the heat. Several families milled around inside. An old woman in mourning white shuffled slowly toward the altar carrying a rough-woven basket with her offering: bananas, a coconut and several sticks of incense.

The shade of the temple was fragrant with sandalwood and frangipani. I relaxed, inhaling the sweet coolness. As my eyes adjusted, I noticed a toddler holding on to his mother's purple sari, peeking out at me with brown saucer eyes. I raised my hand next to my cheek and gave him a tiny, half-hand wave. He laughed and darted behind his mother. I lifted my fan and started a game of peek-a-boo. I hoped my friendliness would make up for the indiscretion of plopping down into a heap on the temple floor. His mother smiled at me and, as I turned, I saw two teenage girls, elegant in their flowing silk salwar kameez, watching. The taller, bolder one approached.

'Hello,' she said, soft and hesitant at first, casting her eyes toward my hat, then quickly back down to the floor.

'Hello.' I smiled.

'Where from?'

'USA. America.'

'Ah, America.' She brightened. 'What is your name?' She spoke haltingly as though she were trying a well-practised classroom drill.

After our exchange of names the second girl spoke up. 'How you like my country?'

'We adore it. We feel very lucky to be here.' I bucked up, brightening my smile, forgetting my sun-sick exhaustion, trying to be a mini-ambassador. *The world has had enough reasons to hate the US these past few years; I don't want to give them another.*

The first girl opened her hand to reveal a small digital camera. 'Picture?'

'Of course.' I reached for the camera. She hesitated, looking confused.

'No, they want to take a picture with you.' An older boy, a brother I assumed, materialised from the group of pilgrims. Both girls giggled. I couldn't imagine why two exquisite Indian girls wanted their picture taken with a dumpy lady. *It must be my big hat,* I thought, and smiled. For a few minutes at least, I forgot about my burning feet and tired body. I positioned myself behind the two girls, trying to camouflage my limp T-shirt with their flowing gold silk. The girls offered a handshake as we said our goodbyes.

That's when all hell broke loose. Another group of girls, older, rushed over to shake my hand and have a picture; then their brothers joined in, and mothers carrying babies, then toddlers and grandmothers. They all talked at once, thrusting out their hands at me, crowding around. The dads stood back and flashed their cameras. Finally noticing the commotion, Jack sauntered over to take pictures with his camera as well. Then the dads handed their cameras to him and jumped in for more photos. In an instant I was transformed from doddering, clod-footed temple ignoramus to queen for a day.

'Ready to go?' Jack asked after a few more shots.

'Not quite yet,' I said. 'What's the hurry? We have a few more who want pictures.' I turned to two little boys who'd just then summoned the courage to step forward.

Perhaps it was the hat that drew so much attention, I thought, sitting by the pool later that night. Or perhaps not. Maybe it was my stillness. Perhaps my loiterer's pace, forced by illness, offered me the chance to notice more, to appear approachable. Maybe the silver lining of illness opened me to the kind of personal connection that's only possible when we pause.

Anne Sigmon is a Californian writer, stroke survivor, and autoimmune patient who covers adventure travel for people with health limitations. Her stories about travel to remote corners from Burma to Uzbekistan appear regularly in magazines and anthologies. She blogs about autoimmune disease and stroke (www.AnneSigmon.com) and adventure travel (www.JunglePants.com).

Via Ferrata

Hazel Pennington

There just wasn't anywhere to put my foot. With frozen fingers I clung wretchedly to the mountainside, the toe of one alarmingly flexible walking shoe making tenuous contact with a tiny nib of rock, the other probing in vain for a nib lower down. Fine sleet was settling on every small projection as I tried to remember which of the many enthusiastic, fit young people on my walking holiday in the Dolomites had united to persuade me to have a go at an 'easy' *via ferrata*. 'You'll have a brilliant time,' I'd been told, 'and you'll feel perfectly safe.' In truth the only danger I faced was that of acquiring a few bruises – and maybe a dent to my pride. The harness and karabiners attaching me to strong cables bolted to the rock would ensure that if I slipped I would fall only a little way. But somehow that knowledge didn't translate into a feeling of security, as I contemplated the sheer drop to the path far below. Well, all right then, not really that far. Maybe about thirty feet. Far enough. When I had booked the holiday, of all the various activities on offer in these beautiful limestone mountains – energetic walks at all levels, wildflower walks, painting walks, and an exploration of the precipitous slopes and ridges where the *Alpini* troops lived out much of the First World War, and during those years fixed a system of cables and ladders to the rock – the only one I could guarantee

I wouldn't be trying was a via ferrata. Climbing in any form was absolutely not for me.

So how on earth had I been talked into it? I think the explanation lay in the stimulation of being with a group of strangers, mostly considerably younger than me, all eagerly sharing their experiences every evening over dinner. Their enthusiasm was infectious. And during the few days I'd been there I'd already done three high-level walks and survived, even though one narrow path had been along a mountainside steep enough to merit a cable to hold. When someone told me the cable was part of the via ferrata network, the whole concept seemed suddenly less scary. With something to hang on to, how hard could it be?

Then the First World War walk had taken us into a tunnel hollowed out by troops, which led along the top of a high ridge. Observation posts allowed us to see across the sheer-sided valley to the faint line of a path partway up the mountainside, which seemed from where we were crouching to be a smooth, vertical rock wall. Learning that men had lived night and day, winter and summer, on these narrow ridges and hair-raisingly steep slopes, constructing dugouts and stores, hauling heavy equipment, taking messages, carrying supplies up and bodies down, all the while under threat of enemy fire, made the idea of trying out a via ferrata for a couple of hours on a summer's day pale into insignificance.

Climbing up in the sunshine had been just the right side of exciting, a new experience, and a new skill taught to us with kindly patience by the two guides. We learned how to use our karabiners, always ensuring that one remained attached to the cable as we moved past bolts holding the cable to the rock, and how to let someone descending on the same cable pass safely.

The view from the top was tremendous, and for the twenty minutes or so we were allowed to relax up there, I tried not to think about the inevitable descent. Then suddenly, it seemed, the sky clouded over, sleet began to fall, and everyone was on the move.

To start with, the descent wasn't difficult. For a while we walked down a rocky path. But the last section resembled Beachy Head, a sheer drop. Idiotically, on that bright summer morning, I hadn't thought to bring gloves; my hands were going numb, and the sleet was turning everything slippery.

'I'm stuck,' I said in a small voice.

Carla, above me on the rock waiting patiently for me to descend so that she could move, relayed the message up to one of our unfeasibly youthful guides. A moment later Sam, all downy skin and stylish single earring, had clambered effortlessly past Carla and materialised beside me. Down on the path a couple of hours ago I had wanted to pat him on the head and offer him a sweetie. Now he was my saviour. He scrutinised the rock below for a toehold and gently talked me down. Was I imagining it or did an unearthly radiance surround him?

Half an hour later, after a brisk walk, we were all safely sitting in a *rifugio*, clutching mugs of hot chocolate, and sharing our tales of derring-do. I wasn't the oldest in the party. Mike, looking all of a debonair sixty, was celebrating his seventieth birthday by trying his first via ferrata climb. As you do.

If I'd thought that, having managed eventually to complete the climb, I was now just one of the crowd, I was disabused of this notion on the way back down to the road. A young student from Indonesia, whom I'd noticed shyly watching me several times on the climb, finally plucked up courage to talk to me.

'May I ask, how old are you?' she asked.

'Sixty-three,' I replied, smiling encouragingly at her.

'Sixty-three?' A touch of emotion crept into her voice. 'Oh, you are my inspiration!' she said reverently.

It seemed perhaps I was an old lady after all.

Hazel Pennington grew up in Lancashire, then worked as a systems analyst, a teacher of languages and finally a bike tour organiser. Now living in Bath, she spends a lot of time walking, gardening, cycling and rowing. Other interests include reading, music, sustainable living, travel, meeting new people and trying new experiences.

Taking the Plunge
Matthew Parris

First, don't try this at home. It could have ended in disaster. It was ignorant and it was dangerous

But it was not impetuous. I have been thinking, talking, and finally fretting about swimming across the River Thames for fifteen years, since in my forties I moved into a flat on Narrow Street in the East End of London, looking out over the river at Limehouse Reach. I watched twenty-foot tides racing up and down the river. Swans, cormorants, traffic cones and sometimes corpses floated by. Barges, sailing ships, warships, cruise liners, disco-boats and police launches buzzed, roared or chugged past my balcony, day and night.

Except at my favourite time. In the small hours of the morning the river is silent, alone with itself, slapping and sucking at the foreshore beneath my balcony. This would be the time to swim across, with no shipping and nobody to raise an alarm.

I'm no great swimmer but I can stay afloat. I would make my crossing in high summer when the water was warmest; and at high tide, as it turned. I would start from the stairs at Globe Wharf on the other side and swim straight across to the Ratcliff Cross stairs at Narrow Street. And I would do it without a boat or any kind of flotation in tow, because otherwise it isn't real. I started telling friends my plan.

But somehow I never got around to executing it. The years passed; I turned fifty, then fifty-five. Friends would yawn as I insisted I'd do it. Sometimes someone would say 'how about tonight?' – and I'd be momentarily keen, then reflect that the tide wasn't right, I needed to be fresh for the morning… or whatever.

Sometimes on a warm day I'd test the temperature. Fine. So was I getting cold feet? The talk continued, however, the plans for how the lodger Tom would flash a light on the balcony across the river so I'd know the coast was clear… oh yes, this would surely happen. But somehow never tonight, never this month, never this year. The deferral was becoming Chekhovian.

In a couple of weeks I shall turn sixty-one. London has been hot. Online tide tables said there would be high tides, midweek, in the small hours. My partner (fiercely opposed) was away. 'Come on,' I thought: 'do it.' I told an LSE student, Jonathan, who's working for me. 'I'll come too,' he said. High tide, 03.35 on Thursday morning. Tom would be there on balcony duty. Supper, a few hours' sleep, then…

Astonishing, how fearful I then became. How had I got myself into this? Why hadn't I kept my mouth shut? Now I understood the subliminal reason I'd never done it before. All that thinking about it and boasting about it had scared me. At midnight, as I lay my head on the pillow, at first sleep would not come.

It's being woken in the dark that's worst. I donned trunks and an old singlet to swim in, and some discardable flip-flops. We stood on the balcony. The river was very black. We called a minicab just after 3 a.m., to take us under the nearby Rotherhithe tunnel to the other side. We crept down the Globe stairs wordlessly, so as not to alert any flat-dwellers, and undressed. Each wondered if he'd be going ahead if it wasn't for the other.

But from my balcony came no flashing light. Could Tom not see us? A big barge slid past heading (surprisingly fast) upstream. Then my balcony light flashed. We struck out for the other side.

There's a kind of relief, once you start. The water was choppy but not too cold, and I could feel no current. We swam silently, breast-stroke, surprised at the ease. Except that across the water, perspectives were altering unaccountably. Then I saw trees moving behind the buildings on the other side. Why? When I turned to look for Globe Stairs behind us, they were far over to our right. We were being carried upstream. Fast. The tide was still coming in. Fast.

We decided to stay close together, not to fight the current, and keep swimming towards the opposite bank: hard work now in the choppy water. I saw a flashing blue light moving towards us from our left. 'River Police!' I hissed. No, a light on a buoy; and we were being swept towards it. Soon we were almost past the King Edward VII Park and approaching Wapping. In the first glimmer of dawn we saw sailing dinghies, moored offshore. Jonathan managed to grab a rope, and I a rudder.

We were breathless, and getting cold. We could see the stilts of a riverside boardwalk some way away, near the Prospect of Whitby pub in Wapping. If we could just reach those stilts before being swept further... We struck out. Jonathan, at twenty the stronger swimmer, did it easily. I just did it, and in doing so, understood how easily and fast you can lose heart in fast-flowing cold water. We pulled our way round to a little creek, plunged across and climbed a high iron ladder, onto a road. We had been in the water for perhaps half an hour.

For a moment I felt weak and shaky, my balance thrown, and began to shiver. We were about three-quarters of a mile upriver from Limehouse. The park was locked. No way home but up onto a big road, the Highway, back from the river. We were barefoot, and Jonathan in only skimpy underpants. 'Let's run,' he said.

We flew, pounding the pavements barefoot, I feeling strangely lightheaded, my normal limp gone. It was like a dream. My brain raced. GMT! Navigational tables are in GMT! High tide would have been at 04.35, not 03.35. We pounded on. A passing man jumped, frightened, away.

And soon we were in Narrow Street, ringing the doorbell. 'You disappeared,' said Tom. 'We saw you go in, then nothing.' He hadn't called the police: 'What could they do? I doubted you'd drowned.'

I stopped shivering. The shower (so much mud!) was sublime. The sweet tea was nectar. The sleep was heavenly.

But it was the waking up on Thursday that felt transfigurative. Yes! I did it! I can do it. And I'll never have to do it again.

Matthew Parris worked for the Foreign Office and the Conservative Research Department before serving as MP for West Derbyshire. He now writes as a columnist and occasional travel writer for *The Times* and *The Spectator*, broadcasts for radio and television and is the author of *Inca Kola*, recounting his backpacking adventures in Peru. The piece above was originally published in *The Times* in 2010.

Atlas Traverse

Chris Wright

We had always gone back to Morocco. When we were in our early twenties, with 'alternative' travel companies Magic Bus or Sun Dance. With our three kids before we all drove across the Sahara. With the same kids, by then in their teens, in a battered Peugeot with three rows of seats. When the kids had flown the nest, though one of them tagged along with us for a week or so. In a camper van when we no longer had my parents to look after.

Now it was just me. My wife had died after a car crash and I had suffered seat belt injuries and had lost part of my bowel. Yet still Morocco called.

The last time we had gone together, Jan had not been well and we had fought long and hard about the mountains. I wanted to drive the tracks and trek the peaks of the Atlas; it might be my last opportunity to do so. Jan was less keen on the high and wild places. So this time I would do what I wanted. I had the licence. I was on my own.

It was May and snow lay thick on the High Atlas. It was a few weeks too early for Toubkal, the highest mountain in north Africa, so I settled on Mgoun, the second highest peak.

Installed in a small and basic hotel in the Bouguemez Valley, the trail-head, I negotiated with Houcine, a French-speaking guide. We soon established that the muleteers would not take their precious animals up Mgoun because of the snow but I could consider an east-west traverse in the foothills. As we were not going up the mountain and I was alone, we agreed that having both guide and muleteer was an extravagance. The muleteer, Mohammed, would carry food and bags on his mule and would act as guide as well as cook. The complication was that we would not share a language, but then life is pretty basic in the hills and we both thought we would manage.

Houcine and I identified the trek on the map and in the guidebook and talked about the middle stretch, where there were no obvious stopping places between day two and three. 'The muleteer is in charge of where you stop; he knows best; he knows everybody,' he insisted. I nodded agreement and acceptance.

Introductions were made and I slept early to be ready for the early morning start.

The first day was long but uneventful. With only a day bag to carry, I managed the walking along dusty mountain tracks with no problem. When we deserved a break, Mohammed spread a blanket and served lunch from the saddle bags: tinned fish and salad with yesterday's bread and the ubiquitous mint tea of the Atlas, served sickly sweet with sugar for energy. Night time brought us to a caravanserai, a place for travellers on mule or on foot. There was little conversation but the man who ran the place sidled up to me in the morning and, perhaps with an eye to my white hair, warned me, 'You have a long day ahead.'

Though a little stiff from the first day, I strode off without a care. After a couple of hours the track and the stream became one and, in sign language, Mohammed told me to change to plastic sandals. For the first hour or so I delighted in the cool snow melt water running over my toes. Mohammed kept his own feet dry by jumping athletically from rock to rock or by running along the hillside and then calling the mule so that he could jump on its back to cross the stream.

We passed the last village before the high pass. This was the second day, when Mohammed would know a place to stay. He must know someone at the far end of the village, I assured myself. The track and stream turned into the mountains and we began to climb steeply towards the pass. What had been cool water between my toes now became a bit of a pain. My feet had softened after several hours in the water and my soles had to grip the sandals hard. I gestured to Mohammed that it was time to put my boots back on but he shook his head and pointed to the water.

As the entire soles of my feet were beginning to turn into two huge blisters, it was with a sinking heart that I began to understand Mohammed's solution to the accommodation problem. He was intending to run days two and day three together and then rest up on the far side of the pass. An obvious solution for a mountain man – but not one appreciated by an old fellow with blistered feet.

We crossed the pass at nine thousand feet. I had eventually been allowed to put my boots back on – after all, the stream couldn't flow over the top of the pass – but the damage was done. Every step was painful and my legs were cramping on the descent, a reaction to the tensing of the muscles to grip my sandals on the way up.

I barely made the caravanserai before dusk fell. I knew my duty was to help Mohammed unload the heavy saddle bags but I could hardly stand. I waved away any discussion of dinner and collapsed on the foam mattress that had been put down for me. When I awoke in the night, I had to think long and hard about the process of getting to my feet. They felt as if I had been given the bastinado, a beating on the soles of the feet, and spasmed wildly as I touched the ground. My thigh muscles went into spasm as if in competition.

Next morning, one of the waiters sidled up to me. 'Your track is blocked. There is too much water.' Our language did not stretch to much more and Mohammed looked at me questioningly.

'Let's go and see,' I suggested, but he was reluctant.

'Ring Houcine,' he said, gesturing towards my mobile phone. It was reassuring but unreal to talk to Houcine.

'They say the track is blocked.'

'What do you want to do?'

I thought of the high pass and knew my feet did not want to go back the way we had come.

'There is another road.'

'Let's take that.' I handed the phone to Mohammed.

We turned south and walked through the mountains for two days; nothing too demanding. It was high country but we had already made the height gain and never really lost it again. Early on the second day Mohammed brought me to a small inn in a village high above the plain. 'Tomorrow there is a bus to Ouarzazate.' I paid him his tip and in a flash he was astride the mule, riding back to his family.

I had done my traverse. Not an east-west traverse as we had intended but a north-south traverse across the main ridge of the Atlas. Ouarzazate is eleven hours' travelling by bus back across the Atlas from our intended destination, Demnate, all the way round via Marrakech.

I laid up for several days drinking coffee '*nous-nous*' (strong but milky, half and half), waiting for my feet not to scream each time I offered them to the ground. Then I turned my face towards Toubkal. It was time.

Chris Wright is based in Yorkshire and reaches out from there to the world, travelling widely in Europe, Asia and Africa. He has driven the Sahara and spent thirteen family years in Portugal. The place he always returns to is Morocco, his spiritual home. During a  night under the African stars a Tanzanian night watchman solemnly shared the sentiment: 'We are all together.'

A Grave Matter

James McCarthy

In April 1933, a large limousine stopped in a cloud of dust outside the walls of the ancient holy city of Mecca in Saudi Arabia. Together with her driver and an equerry, out stepped the petite figure of sixty-six-year-old Lady Evelyn Zainab Murray Cobbold. This aristocratic daughter of an ancient and well-connected Scottish family was dressed from head to foot in the all-enveloping Muslim *burqa*, with only a few slits at eye level to enable her to take in the scene – the culmination of a life-long devotion to the Muhammadan faith.

Her family had extensive estates on Harris in the Outer Hebrides: her father, Charles Adolphus Murray, 7th Earl of Dunmore, purchased the fine shooting estate of Glencarron in Wester Ross, where his daughter established a reputation as an accomplished deer stalker and salmon fisher, maintaining these interests right up into her latter years. She was not loath to use her aristocratic associations, not least to smooth the path of her travels in the Middle East.

She certainly required these when she became the first known Western woman to make the *Hajj* and penetrate the Holy City, albeit that the pilgrimage was made in some style, contrasting with the considerable discomforts of many other pilgrims who had made arduous journeys from around the globe. Through the good offices of the distinguished Arabist Harry St John Philby, a close friend of the greatly respected King Ibn Saud, the normal requirement for Europeans to spend a year in the city of Medina was waived in her case and she obtained a rare interview with his son, Amir Faysal, in addition to being received by the Pasha of Meknes and two sheikhs.

All of this was greatly helped by her fluency in Arabic and friendship with Philby: it enabled her to make convivial visits to the women's quarters at Medina and Mecca (accompanied by two eunuchs) and to provide valuable first English descriptions of their lives and culture, recorded in her book *Pilgrimage to Mecca*. Not surprisingly, Lady Cobbold became something of an icon within the Muslim community in Britain and elsewhere, and was given the honour, following her pilgrimage, of delivering a speech to mark the birthday of the Prophet Muhammad at the Carlton Hotel in London on 14th December 1933. She died in 1963, aged ninety-six, and was buried on a hillside on her estate, according to Muslim custom. But the record suggests there was something of a problem.....

In mid 2007, researching the lives of Scottish travellers, I made contact with a number of Lady Cobbold's descendants and a Muslim convert, Yakub Zaki, alias Dr James Dickie of Greenock, a considerable Arabic scholar, currently compiling a book on British Muslims. He was concerned that Lady Cobbold might not in fact be facing Mecca: if she was seriously out of alignment, she might have to be disinterred for the peace of her everlasting soul. There was only one way of determining this, which was to locate the grave, using a special *Qibla* compass, on which the direction of Mecca from any city in the world can be determined. As Dr Dickie's compass instructions were in Arabic, I had to find my own.

I located the Edinburgh Central Mosque's car park keeper in his little hut behind the mosque, where an amiable attendant purveyed a variety of goods (in addition to selling car park tickets) including the compass, with instructions in fractured English, which by a little bazaar bargaining I purchased for a one-pound reduction.

Glencarron in Wester Ross lies sixty miles west of the Highland capital of Inverness and indications were that the gravesite was accessible from the very scenic Inverness to Kyle of Lochalsh railway line via a rough track of about six miles into the mountains to the southeast. Deciding to be independent, I eschewed the offer of a four-wheel drive by the estate stalker and opted for pedal power. An early train start saw me passing the Cairngorms range by late morning, where I experienced the usual lift of the heart at the sight of the far corries and that intangible northern atmosphere conveyed by shining lochans and deep green forest alongside the track – the magic of the boreal forest of pine and swaying birch.

The changeover to the Kyle line, despite a loaded pushbike, was painless. Obviously proud of his two-coach train trundling self-importantly across the sweeps of heather moorland, the eyes of the conductor lit up when he saw my ticket.

'Och, this will make the driver's day when I will tell him that we will be stopping at Achnashellach – and with a pedal bicycle too…!'

Achnashellach is one of those remote stops by special request, and it seems that the driver does not get many requests. The conductor was unsure whether the platform was on the north or south side – important for disembarking the loaded bike – and had to look up his railway 'bible'.

A signals failure at Garve prompted an invitation to passengers to stretch their legs while the driver had a cup of coffee, and the excited young conductor gave me a detailed situation report on what a narrow shave we had had – a few minutes later out of Inverness and 'we might haaf been held up for half an hour! Would you believe, sir, that the incoming train from Invergordon haas by now been stuck for twenty minutes!' His ticket machine bounced on his paunch in his wonderment.

The Achnashellach stop, under the shadow of a lowering mountain, fringed by a wet mass of dripping rhododendron, turned out to be a blue wooden shed capable of sheltering two slim persons (*'It is an offence to permit smoking in this waiting space – offenders will be prosecuted – by order'*) but I was the sole passenger alighting – not without difficulty, given the drop of several feet to the platform with an unevenly-balanced bicycle. A steep dirt track, overhung by oak woods sheltering ancient vehicles in various states of decay, led to the main road.

The railway line passed a few yards from the main door of Gerry's Hostel, which led into the essential drying room and the main dormitory of about ten metal bunk beds. The dining-cum-sitting room was dominated by a large original metal grate with open fire, while from the rafters hung various unidentifiable animal skins. A hot water tank was insulated by swathes of antique newspapers, while a store of canned food was offered at marked prices. Bookcases housed well-thumbed magazines and periodicals such as *National Geographic* in complete runs going back to the late 1960s. Many empty whisky bottles, some of quality malts, provided appropriate decoration on mantelpiece and shelves.

When he arrived, Gerry appeared like a latter-day Ben Gunn, grey-bearded and in that Highland uniform, a pair of stout Wellingtons. I was advised that I was the only occupant of the dormitory: Gerry inhabited another part of the house. After a solitary supper, I read of the adventures of other residents in the route book, many coming for winter climbing in this mountainous territory. I retired early in preparation for a vigorous day, but awoke after a nightmare concerning a recent entry:

'11 p.m. John not back – called police and Mountain Rescue Team. Found with a broken leg after falling off his bike in the dark.'

The route he had taken was my own on the morrow…

That morrow turned out to be grey and damp, with the cloud base down to about five hundred feet – perfect for biting midges. I managed to heave my bicycle over the padlocked gate at the crossing over the railway. But a mile up the track, I was stymied by a much more serious locked gate about eight feet high in the deer fence which stretched across the valley. Climbing this with one hand and a bike in the other – not to mention an artificial hip and two screws holding the other seventy-one-year-old femur in place – was out of the question; frustrated, I was obliged to continue on foot. I had also discovered that the midges preferred a stationary target. That deer fence was in fact giving essential protection for a fine remnant of the old Caledonian pine forest which clothed the steep banks of the gorge known as the Sloc Mor, or 'Great Gorge', the scattered trees providing a fine contrast to the surrounding heather moorland, now in full purple bloom.

On either side of the track, mosses of a great variety of hues from emerald to wine were interspersed with bog-cotton, the purple field scabious and the insectivorous butterwort which clung to the wettest banks, while the gold of bog asphodel alternated with tough deer grass. In this vast amphitheatre of silence (I saw no-one during the whole day) the thunder of waterfalls flowing into the Allt a' Chonais could be heard half a mile away at the great Coire Leathad an Tobair.

On my left, the massive split crags of Sgurr nan Ceannaichean were swathed in wreaths of typical Scotch mist, drifting like smoke across this classic U-shaped glen, with its scattered glacial moraines on either side of the river. Even without sun, the damp made everything shine verdantly. The only living things I saw in several hours of walking were a pair of croaking ravens, ominously circling like vultures above my head.

My notes said that the gravesite was to be found on the northern hillside a short way before the shooting lodge at Glenuaig, and after a walk of about five miles from the deer fence and a short steep climb through the sodden grass and heather, that is where I found it: one upright headstone marking the grave of Lady Cobbold's grandson, Squadron Leader Algernon 'Toby' Sladen, and a smaller one alongside, apparently broken off from its concreted plinth, above a horizontal slab pointing up the glen.

An inset bronze plaque with an inscription from Chapter XXII of the Koran had been deliberately scored, and the broken headstone seemed maliciously damaged. The inscription read 'Lady Evelyn Cobbold 1867–1963 Daughter of the 7th Earl of Dunmore Widow of John Dupuis Cobbold'. I retired to a shed, thoughtfully provided by the estate for benighted ramblers, behind the lodge to munch my oatcakes and cheese and contemplate what had happened on 31st January 1963.

That winter was the coldest on record. Severe frost which lasted for weeks left the ground like concrete. When Lady Cobbold died in a nursing home in Inverness, the family were aware of her final instructions to be buried according to Muslim custom, i.e. in a recumbent position facing Mecca. While not specifying a location, she wanted to be placed where deer graze – what better place than a remote hillside near to her Glenuaig shooting lodge? No Christian minister was to be present, but the appropriate Arabic prayers were to be said, and a verse from the Koran was to be inscribed on the gravestone. For this purpose, an Imam, Sheikh Muhammad Tufail, was summoned from the Islamic Cultural Centre in London, who travelled by overnight sleeper and was transported by car from Inverness to the estate.

On the day, a solemn cavalcade of four-wheeled vehicles bore about forty people, many from the noble families of Britain, up the rutted track from the main house at Glencarron Lodge (where Lord Dunmore had insisted that the railway company provide a 'halt by request' for residents and guests to the estate). It was bitterly cold and there were flurries of icy snow as some of the fitter mourners clambered up the hillside to where the *ghillie* and deerstalker had previously dug the grave. According to the Muslim record of the event:

'… This Lady was a woman of great power and autonomy, and was a typical example of that class of aristocracy of Scotland who are fiercely proud of their blood, descent and Scottish nationality, and consider the English to be inferior. Accordingly, just as Lady Cobbold fully demonstrated in her will that she was a Muslim, she also maintained in it the Scottish aristocratic tradition that the coffin was to be followed by a bagpiper playing "lamentful tunes"… Sheikh Tufail said the funeral prayer, and uttered it loudly so that the gathering may be aware that it was in Arabic.'

It would have been a surreal sight, with the Imam's robes blowing in the icy wind, the air filled with his high-pitched Arabic prayers and the piper's 'lamentful tunes' while the noses of the assembled gentry became bluer than their claimed blood in the bitter snow showers, all against a backdrop of sullen crags.

Although the grave was dug in the direction of the glen, which was roughly east-facing, it appears that the Imam was doubtful about its orientation. According to local legend, he did not understand the responses of the gravediggers – given the conditions of their labours, no doubt in four-letter Gaelic words – but eventually agreed to the internment.

Back at the lodge, where refreshment was taken in the Scottish tradition, some of the same nobility insisted on referring to the Imam as the 'emu', no doubt wondering what to offer him as a devout Muslim.

Using my *Qibla* compass I reckoned the grave was pointing east-northeast – about six degrees off the correct direction. Somehow, after such an adventurous life, with her body resting in the peaceful Highland scenery, it seemed unimportant. I was relieved to be able to let sleeping dames lie...

The five-mile trudge back to the deer fence seemed even longer than before and the rain started in earnest. I took heed of the notice 'At your own risk' beside the bridge over the river which consisted of two slender wires – one to hold, and the other to slide feet along. The downhill bike ride to the still deserted hostel was almost a pleasure.

Disinclined to face my own cooking, I opted for supper at the Strathcarron Hotel, but the nine-mile ride, after an active day, tested my weary legs. The hotel was jumping, full of young people on a Saturday night apparently trying to get drunk in the shortest possible time (from the number of kilts on large shaggy men, there may have been a function) and a large-screen television blaring out in a corner. It provided something of a contrast with the absolute solitude of the day. The long ride back in wind-driven rain in pitch darkness ensured that I slept like the proverbial log that night, undisturbed by the ghostly creakings of no doubt long-dead hillwalkers.

Following military service in Kenya, **James McCarthy** undertook forest exploration in Uganda and Tanzania. Awarded several prestigious fellowships, he is a joint winner of the International Proverse Prize for his life of Sir George Macartney. He retired as Deputy Director (Scotland) of the Nature Conservancy Council in 1991.

Trek China Challenge
Diana Moran

In our bright pink T-shirts, we were all shapes, sizes and ages, but at seventy I was the eldest. All strangers to one another, we had signed up to Breast Cancer Care's 'Trek China Challenge', a sponsored endurance test along the Great Wall of China. I was ready for the journey of a lifetime which was to test my fitness.

On arrival in Beijing, we whizzed along busy motorways past skyscrapers and industrial areas, then on spanking new roads planted with acres of spindly fir trees. It was cold and dark on arrival at Simatai mountain lodge and facilities were basic. After the welcome briefing I retired to bed in a dormitory for four, with a damp and very smelly bathroom. Donning warm pyjamas and despite the hard bed, I soon fell asleep, grateful for the hot water bottle I'd packed at the very last minute.

After a substantial breakfast, we made packed lunches and collected our day's water supply of four bottles each. At 7.30 a.m. we met in the courtyard, dressed in our trekking clothes. Most carried at least one walking stick, with a rubber end to protect the ancient Wall. We were cold and apprehensive, tired from the ten-hour flight and time change. I took it upon myself to lead an impromptu warm-up followed by muscle stretches.

We thirty-two trekkers were divided into two groups, each

accompanied by a representative of the charity, a Chinese doctor and a Chinese guide who spoke good English. We were driven to our starting point, Gubeikou, and had our first experience of Chinese public loos: footprints and a smelly hole. There would be no toilet facilities at all along the Wall; setting your rucksack in the middle of the track denoted you were off in the bushes. As we were about to set off, the heavens opened and soaked us. I jumped into my protective clothing.

The Wall wasn't as I had expected, but a narrow track high up in the mountain peaks, unkempt, exposed, daunting and precarious. Known as the Great Dragon, it stretches thousands of miles across the north of China, from Qinhuangdao on the Yellow Sea to Jiayuguan near the Mongolian border; it switchbacks through seventeen provinces, from Shanghai Pass (Old Dragon's Head) by the Pacific Ocean to the salt lake sand marshes of Lop Nur, where it finally lays its writhing tail to rest. It would take about three hundred days to walk its entire length, but none of us had that time to spare, so six very different sections had been selected.

Construction of the Wall, built as a fortification against the Mongols, began two thousand years ago. It snaked over rocky summits, through leafy valleys and across stony deserts, and legend has it that thousands of inadequately clothed and fed soldiers perished of cold, disease or starvation, their bodies cast into the foundations, giving it a grim reputation as the longest cemetery in the world.

We trekked through wind and rain, the ground uneven and wild with gradients of up to seventy degrees, much of the Wall derelict, strewn with rubble, overgrown with vegetation and without a parapet. Sure-footed 'hello people' – Mongolian peasants named for their habit of introducing themselves with a cheery 'hello' – appeared from nowhere and for a few yuan offered a steadying hand in times of trouble. After a picnic lunch we climbed down and trudged through farming villages with terraces carved into the hillside, bursting with ripe maize. We trekked for over five hours, taking in twenty-three of the twelve hundred watchtowers, and at Jinshanling our waiting coach transferred our weary bodies back to the lodge.

Somehow on Day Two, we staggered on through another forty-three watchtowers, following a rough track with steps that were inconsistent – high and low, narrow or shallow – designed to deter enemies, who were never able to achieve a regular, constant rhythm to their step. Nothing had prepared me for the rough and precipitous terrain. A break presented us with the challenge of descending a sheer rock face via three vertical, rusty ladders. This was in order to make our way across a suspended wooden plank bridge, which swayed a thousand feet above a narrow gorge with a silver ribbon of river below. To complete the ordeal we leapt off the far rock face, suspended in a canvas seat harness, to cross the gorge via a terrifying zip wire.

Next day the weather looked bright for our trek; our main luggage would be transferred by coach whilst we tackled the Wall. Many fellow trekkers had experienced breast cancer, as I had twenty-five years ago, so we shared personal stories. The views became more and more dramatic as we trekked, eventually descending into Mongolia through farming areas and arriving at the small village of Gangfang where local folk going about their chores paused to watch us. We called out *Ni hao*, 'hello', and they shyly smiled back.

The Great Dragon had originally been built to keep foreigners out; now it encouraged us in. A visit to the local primary school had been pre-arranged so we arrived with sweets, crayons and colouring books for the children. Happy and bright-eyed, they were intrigued to see 'Big Noses', as they call us Westerners, and giggled and nudged one another. On our arrival at Wuzoulou Lodge, colourful lights, inviting kitchen smells and a bonfire gave a warm welcome. Bizarrely, Elvis songs sounded in the dark night and we responded by impromptu singing and dancing, but our guides advised us that the next day would be hard.

The trek started at three hundred metres above sea level, scrabbling upwards for over three hours with some difficulty. We watched out for one another, lending a hand or moral support. One fall would have sent us tumbling, possibly taking others down too. Long trekking trousers protected against prickly undergrowth as we picked, heaved and clawed our way up difficult paths and rocks. A young member of our group cheekily called out, 'If Granny can do it, we can!' Feeling elated, we stopped to enjoy magnificent views of gorges and reservoirs.

It was exhilarating to be at the top, at eleven hundred metres, where isolated watchtowers now dominated the mountain ridges. This was the last part of the Wall, built in the Ming Dynasty. After several more towers we descended on a different, more exposed route, watching every step. One trekker opted for help from a 'hello man' who guided her but unknowingly became a source of amusement. In rural China it is considered perfectly normal to rid oneself of wind or flatulence by belching or farting without conscience, as this young man demonstrated all day long.

That night neither cold nor cockroaches stopped us from gratefully hitting the sack. Next morning, we climbed through shrubs and undergrowth, squeezing through crevices in rocks and picking through dark caves before starting a scary, rock-climbing descent to

Black Dragon Pool, surrounded by huge rocks and silent but for the fall of water from the mountaintop.

The day was warm, bright and sunny for our final trek at Mutianyu. This section has been renovated to its original grandeur and is popular with tourists who come from Beijing to 'Walk the Great Wall of China'. Views are spectacular, with a cable car to get visitors to the Wall with minimum effort. There was no such luxury for us. This climb was particularly strenuous and exhausting, an awesome final challenge ending with a long, steep incline and the ascent of the dramatic thousand steps of the 'Stairway to Heaven'. It felt more like hell, but our intensive training paid off and reaching the summit was the culmination of our physical and emotional challenge. Our tearful group hugged one another with a mixture of congratulations and relief, thrilled we'd achieved our goal.

After a safe but terrifying descent we looked around the market at base camp, too tired to haggle. We climbed aboard our coach and slept through our journey to Beijing. Following a wonderful shower in a hotel we were transported to the local massage parlour, where we sat en masse, aching feet in bowls of mineral water, whilst a team of delightful young male masseurs simultaneously worked on our exhausted bodies. We finished with reflexology for our tired feet – now that's what I call heaven.

Despite our physical exhaustion we eagerly took in the colourful nightlife of the capital and my eyes got bigger as I strolled down Snack Street where all tastes are catered for with a variety of snakes, centipedes, eels, beetles and scorpions on offer. I reflected that the earlier rural landscape had been surprisingly quiet and I had seen little or no animal or insect life; presumably it had all been eaten.

We took the opportunity over the following days to see sights such as Tiananmen Square, the Forbidden City and the Summer Palace. Then we glammed up for a Gala Supper of traditional Peking Duck and a hilarious, unofficial awards ceremony where we reflected on our Trek China Challenge. We had laughed, cried and been terrified. Our fitness and endurance had been tested and we had raised £200,000 for a wonderful charity.

And I received the award for the 'stretchiest person'.

Diana Moran is an all-round television and radio personality known as the Green Goddess and part of the original team which in February 1983 launched BBC Breakfast TV. Her successful career as fitness guru, author and broadcaster specialising in well-  being, health and ageing issues has spanned four decades. She is an experienced and humorous motivational speaker.

Canoeing the Severn

Libby James

We had known each other since school days, the sort of friendship that you can happily pick up after several years of neglect, and we both fancied a challenge. Jay had a canoe and wanted to take it for an adventure; I wanted to see if I could canoe and wild camp. We were both over sixty and our mission was 'to boldly go' – we just weren't sure how far. Our bemused husbands watched our plans gather together.

We set off from the weir at Shrewsbury, our canoe laden with tent, sleeping bags, stove, pots, food, water, change of clothes and trowel (don't ask). Jay was assigned to rear steerage, Libby on front point, both of us wearing life jackets that masked waists and crept up, thus removing our necks – very attractive. A plastic milk bottle bobbed along behind the canoe, keeping cool in the water, attached by a grubby piece of binder twine.

I had printed off directions from a website that gave lots of tips for canoe touring on the River Severn; the sun was shining and we felt very pleased with ourselves. Approaching the first island, I read our first direction – 'Goffs Island – pass left' – and we confidently headed down on the left side of the island, much to the bemusement of a nearby angler as we limboed under a massive tree trunk and fought our way past greenery back to the river proper. At the next direction – 'Pimley Island – left' – again I felt we should follow instructions and we fought our way through vegetation, emerging with bits of tree embedded in our hair. I reread the instructions carefully and decided they meant us to pass the islands on our left shoulder: in other words, use the other side.

We paddled under a railway bridge and a train passed overhead, Telford bound. An hour and a half later we managed to escape the meanders of Shrewsbury that would have taken us five minutes by car and paddled for Atcham, past Paradise Meadow where playgroups of young geese were herded along by nanny geese. After seven miles of paddling we pulled up just past Atcham's bridges on a pebbly beach and had lunch, looking across at the beautiful sandstone church where Geraint and I got married a few years ago. We drank our tea and headed off downstream for an hour and a half, only to find Atcham church tower still looming ahead over the trees.

This was a slow journey of chat and splash of oars. We met kingfishers, flycatchers, buzzards, swallows, swifts, thrushes and tiny unnameable warblers, our view mostly closed in by bushes and trees that opened up unexpectedly to frame sandstone cliffs.

Spotting a possible tea-brewing site, we pulled across. The problem, we quickly discovered, was how to disembark onto a steep, slightly muddy bank when the canoe was in fairly deep water and our balance was not very balanced; but we were determined. We struggled inelegantly, ending up in a tangled mess on the bank, covered in goose poo and in fits of giggles. At least we'd escaped a dunking. We had our tea, admired a different church spire, Wroxeter, and got back into the canoe with slightly more decorum.

Towards evening we pulled up onto a small beach, disturbing a flock of lapwings, having travelled fifteen-and-a-half miles and needing to stretch out. We set up camp in a green field, sorted food and as the sun set we snuggled into our sleeping bags to read, expecting to be up with the larks. Instead, we were still supine at eight-thirty next morning. But, kettle on, breakfast and ablutions made, camp repacked, trowel used, we were soon on the water and heading towards the Buildwas Power Station cooling towers.

The next section consisted of wide meanders through the flood plain, the river flowing over a shallow, sandy bed with stony beaches, sand martins and oystercatchers winging over us. Four canoes laden with lads were our companions along this stretch; furnished with crash helmets, they were on a daytrip to the rapids. We watched them go past us for the final time as we had our sarnies under the Albert Edward Bridge, while a coal train chugged overhead. In the Ironbridge Gorge, we waved at the people along the street and on the iconic cast-iron bridge.

Jackfield Rapids had us nervous with anticipation. Our directions stated they were Grade 3 or 4 in some levels and should be avoided by the less experienced. Just before, we stopped and unloaded the canoe, thinking that we didn't want to be chasing our sleeping bags down the rapids, even if they were in waterproof bags. The customers in the pub garden on the opposite bank all got their cameras out and prepared to watch. We set off paddling like mad, skirting the large back-wave and rock in the middle of the stream and nearly hitting the rocks at the edge. But we made it to the beach below, emptied excess water out and had a celebratory cuppa and piece of cake, bowing to the clapping pub crowd.

We were still congratulating ourselves as we set off again. Jay had changed into a dry sweatshirt, and I'd slipped my water shoes off to let my feet dry. A group of ducks were posing on a tree in the middle of the river and we cockily turned the canoe to photograph them. I took the camera from its dry bag, but the current was strong and we drifted towards a tree – and a big branch pushed Jay out of the canoe and toppled us.

Suddenly we were spluttering and grabbing bags, oars and the canoe. Luckily, the water was only chest-deep.

At the side of the river, standing in deep smelly mud with leeches, we threw our bags out onto the nettles. The food bag, tent bag and Jay's clothes bag had all filled with water. Jay had bashed her knee. I was unscathed but had lost my camera, a sunhat, one water shoe and a glove. We got back aboard and relaunched more nervously, our lifejackets helping keep us warm as we looked in vain for a site to dry out in the thickly wooded valley.

Then the valley opened up and we came to a farm; we pulled in and I went up the riverbank to inspect. There was a just-mown hayfield in the evening sun: perfect. I hopped along the field with one shoe to find the farmer, who took pity on two drowned rats and let us camp. Jay hung her clothes on a tree in the sun and I pegged the tent out to dry. Jay donned my emergency gear, but I'm tall and Jay is not, so my capri trousers were full length on her and my sweatshirt could have fitted two of her; but at least they were dry. Apart from soggy cake our food was fine and the matches were OK. Stretched out on airbeds, drying in the sun, we celebrated with cans of gin and tonic and crisps and olives. I'd brought along an ancient phone that kept its charge for days and we rang our husbands and reassured them we hadn't drowned. A kingfisher flitted by. It was an idyllic spot. As the sun went down, the evening chorus serenaded us from the woods all around, owl hoots included.

Next morning, after a cooked breakfast with the eggs that

survived the turnover, the river was not so tortuous and we paddled down long straight stretches before passing impressive sandstone cliffs and reaching Bridgnorth in time for morning coffee. The canoe grounded near the old bridge and, seeing as Jay had a sore knee, I got out and waded across the stones and the odd glass shard, trying to look nonchalant wearing my remaining water shoe (size eight and black) and one of Jay's (size four and pink). I foraged successfully for coffee while hoping people wouldn't notice my choice of footwear.

In my absence Jay had spoken to a nice young man who ran a canoe hire company and gave us tips for the next section of the river. The current, though shallow, was quite fast. We avoided fishing lines and passed a cute little passenger ferry that manually winched passengers across. The photographic possibilities were endless, but alas, my camera was at one with the Severn! At the pretty town of Arley, the same helpful young man watched our canoe while we bought ice creams, although it had started to drizzle. On re-embarking we were given instructions by the young man (I think he had adopted us) about minor rapids coming up. We set off into the now constant drizzle and met so many anglers we got quite fed up trying to avoid their lines.

At the rapids we charged down the first part, then came to a drop down over a shelf with a reverse wave below – scary since we had a loaded canoe and didn't feel quite so invincible. We paddled like mad again, took a wave over us that soaked our trousers and undies, but our canoe stayed upright. And finally we were at Bewdley.

Lugging canoe and bags up the riverbank in the pouring rain, we waited for our lift, washing our feet in a warm puddle in the car park. As we stripped off to change into dry gear, watched by a couple having a picnic in a car, we felt proud to have paddled forty-four-

and-a-half miles altogether. We'd done it. Would we do it again? Yes! Were we still friends? Yes! Not bad for a couple of gals who were trendy in the seventies…

Libby James is a retired radiographer, enjoying the freedom of the word 'retired'. She lives in Buckinghamshire and loves walking and painting, trying (mainly in an amateur fashion) to capture the scenery she passes through using watercolours and acrylics. Her family and friends keep her sane(ish) and happy.

Solo Cycle around the World

Ann Wilson

So there I was, approaching sixty, retiring early at the end of June, and about to set off alone on the biggest adventure of my life. 'You're very brave,' people kept saying, and I hadn't even left home – I knew I had to earn those words. But funnily enough, no-one called me mad. Perhaps they already knew...

It had all started two years earlier when I told a friend that I'd once cycled from Carlisle to Ipswich and she gave me a book called *A Bike Ride* by Anne Mustoe. This intrepid lady had cycled around the world in 1987 at the age of fifty-four. Little did I know, when I started reading, where it would lead. I found her story so inspiring that within twelve months I'd made up my mind to take a similar journey myself. I would have to quit my job and let out my spare room to pay the bills, but life was suddenly too short for delays – and if Anne could do it, so could I.

Once the decision was made, I spent many hours researching touring bikes and all the equipment I would need – tents, stoves, sleeping bags and the rest. I devoured as many touring cycling books as I could – Dervla Murphy, Alastair Humphreys, Josie Dew – and dozens of online journals. As the departure date approached I did a test ride from Berwick-upon-Tweed to Penrith to remind myself what life on the road was like, and a few circuits of nearby Coniston

Water, but my strategy was to start training in earnest from Calais.

My journey was to take me across western and eastern Europe, parts of the Middle East, India, southeast Asia, the Far East and the USA – twenty countries in all, over a period of fourteen months. I would pedal some 10,500 miles and celebrate my sixtieth birthday in Japan.

Unsurprisingly, not everything went smoothly. It took a while to get used to carrying four laden panniers weighing twenty-two kilos. At the start of the ride, I was such a novice that I had to ask for help to change a tyre. Then disaster struck in Bulgaria when my expensive expedition bicycle was stolen from a cellar lockup while I was couch-surfing with a lovely couple in the capital, Sofia. I replaced it with a much cheaper mountain bike – 'Sofi' – which is still with me to this day. It was either that or give up, and that really wasn't an option.

Except for that incident, I experienced nothing but kindness. Countless strangers gave me food and offered free accommodation, whilst others couldn't do enough to help with directions. Some of the friendships I made have lasted until this day and given me an enduring faith in human nature.

In Iran I experienced the matchless hospitality of the Iranian people when I rolled up to a small town with nowhere to stay. I was immediately offered a room with a local family and introduced to their friends as an honoured guest. With its incredible mountain scenery and exquisite mosques, Iran didn't take long to become my favourite country. To wander round the ruins of Persepolis among only a handful of visitors was one of the greatest privileges of my life.

In India I was again offered food and drink and help with directions – not always accurate but nevertheless well-meant. I saw the fabulous Golden Temple in Amritsar and the holy city of Varanasi on the banks of the Ganges. Halfway across the sub-continent I had the only road accident worth mentioning when I was knocked off my bike by a runaway buffalo, leaving me badly shaken and with a very sore rear. It took six weeks to cross India in the craziest of road conditions, weaving between all kinds of transport and animals – miraculously without further incident – but at some point I was unfortunate enough to pick up the Giardia parasite. I struggled on but eventually succumbed to the illness in Malaysia where I was nursed back to health by a Chinese family. They looked after me for a month and their generosity almost certainly saved me from abandoning the trip altogether.

In Cambodia all sense of dignity was lost when I fell from a boat into the Tonlé Sap River at Siem Reap in front of a party of tourists and their guides. However, the ungraceful dip did nothing to diminish my enjoyment and wonder at the fabulous temples of Angkor Wat.

After biking the length of South Korea I caught a ferry to Kyushu in Japan and continued for nine hundred miles to visit my son in Tokyo. As I rode to meet him, the snow-capped peak of Mount Fuji hanging in the sky was an image which will stay with me forever. From Tokyo I flew to Portland, Oregon in the United States of America and cycled across the continent to visit my brother in Milwaukee.

America displayed its grandeur in many ways – the majestic Columbia River, the Cascade Mountains and the big skies of Montana. In Canada I passed Niagara Falls and rode beside the beautiful Saint Lawrence River. In Montreal, I caught my last flight to a warm welcome in England.

Since returning home, one of the questions I am asked most often is, 'Where did you stay? Did you book ahead?' The answer is that I rarely knew where I was going to spend the night. I carried camping equipment at all times and used it frequently in western Europe and in America. From eastern Europe to southeast Asia accommodation was relatively cheap and campsites few and far between, so I stayed in hotels, hostels, motels and, yes, sometimes 'love hotels'. Maps of any quality were not always easy to find and I often used the size of the font on the map as an indication of whether a place might have a hotel. On the odd occasion I did have to 'wild camp', but this was always the last resort.

Since my solo cycle around the world in 2009–10, I have cycled the Pacific coast of America from Canada to Mexico with four mature cyclists I met in Idaho on my first ride; I've cycled most of the way from Marrakech to Paris and the Danube from Munich to Tbilisi in Georgia.

I'll be celebrating my sixty-fifth birthday cycling home from Estonia via Latvia, Lithuania, Poland, Czech Republic and Germany. And now, I can confidently say I'm an expert on changing a tyre.

Ann Wilson lives in a small market town on the edge of the Lake District and retired from the telecommunications industry in 2009. She has two children and when not travelling the world by bicycle she likes to spend her free time walking the Lakeland Fells.

Wildlife-Watching

Yukon's Ice Bears

Brian Jackman

What was I doing at the age of seventy-eight, sitting in sub-zero temperatures on an Arctic riverbank four thousand miles from home while a grizzly bear – an apex predator with a fearsome reputation – stood within nibbling distance of my outstretched feet?

Bear Cave Mountain Lodge lies within a snowball's throw of the Arctic Circle in the Fishing Branch Protected Area, where the Vuntut Gwitchin First Nation and the regional government have joined hands to set aside 6,500 square kilometres of pristine wilderness as Yukon's largest territorial park.

The accommodation is backwoods basic, but comfort is not what you come here for. The real luxury is the best bear watching in North America, more close up and personal than you ever believed possible, getting to know the animals as individuals in the company of the Yukon's most charismatic guide.

In this land held sacred by the Vuntut Gwitchin, the importance of salmon and grizzly bears is paramount, and visitor numbers are restricted to no more than a handful at any one time. The season is short – just six weeks in which the grizzlies gather to feast on the spawning salmon, piling on the pounds before hibernating in the limestone caverns that honeycomb Bear Cave Mountain – and the Fishing Branch River is the key to it all.

Fed by underground springs, it remains unfrozen all year round, and every autumn 35,000 chum salmon make the 1,500-mile odyssey from the Bering Sea to spawn in its pure waters. At times there are so many fish in the river you feel you could walk across it on their backs without getting your feet wet.

The salmon in turn attract the grizzlies – as many as forty every season – and as they wade through the river an extraordinary transformation takes place. Within minutes their wet fur freezes in the sub-zero temperatures and they become ice bears – and this was the image that had lured me halfway across the world at the age of seventy-eight, hoping to witness this unique natural spectacle myself.

Set in an area the size of Switzerland with only 350 inhabitants, the lodge is unbelievably remote. To reach it I flew north from Vancouver to Dawson City, home of the 1898 Klondike Gold Rush, where the streets are still made of pay dirt and permafrost and the wooden buildings with their false fronts and boardwalks resemble a Spaghetti Western film set.

From here the only access to Bear Cave Mountain was a stunning two-hour helicopter ride across a far-reaching emptiness of deep-frozen rivers and boreal forests bounded by range upon range of chaste white mountains rolling north to the Beaufort Sea.

On we flew, across a roadless desolation of snow-covered tundra known only to the migrating caribou and the wolves that follow them. At last we touched down on the stony shores of the Fishing Branch River to be greeted by Phil Timpany, who runs the lodge, and Smoky, the Norwegian elkhound who is his only companion for much of the time.

Timpany is the 'bear whisperer' of North Yukon. He is to grizzlies what George Adamson was to lions and doesn't even carry a can of pepper spray – the most popular bear deterrent. His weapon of last resort is a 12-gauge pump-action shotgun, but in all his twenty-two years at Bear Cave Mountain he has never had to use it.

On my first morning I grabbed a coffee and stepped out into the bone-clenching chill of a North Yukon dawn. The sky was clear but sun-up was still an hour away as Timpany and I walked down to the river with Smoky at our heels. The lodge is set on a bend of the river with Bear Cave Mountain and its limestone pinnacles on the other side, creating a natural theatre-in-the-round.

Now the stage was set. Locked in an all-embracing silence, we sat on a log at the water's edge and waited for the first bears to arrive as ravens flitted through the trees like souls. The river flowed past us, swift and shallow, its gin-clear waters an angler's dream, alive with the outlines of spawning fish.

Some mornings, said Timpany, he saw moose by the riverside; caribou and wolverine, too; and at night when the aurora borealis swirls and flickers overhead he would hear the eerie harmonies of wolves in the spruce forests.

Even when no bears are in sight their spine-tingling presence is powerful; but we did not have to wait for long. Out of the mist hanging over the river emerged a dark apparition. It was the big male called Stanley, patrolling the riverbank with a rolling swagger as if all this wild land belonged to him. Eleven years old and just entering his prime, he was the spirit of winter made flesh and bone, his heavy coat encased in icicles.

Closer and closer he came until the bear was no more than three paces away from where I sat on the iron-hard ground. 'Good to see you, Stanley,' said Timpany softly as my heartbeat increased a notch or two. But Stanley ignored us completely.

Stanley had evolved an efficient way of catching food that Timpany calls snorkelling, wading along with his head underwater until he spotted his prey, then charging after it in a welter of spray to emerge with a ten-pound fish in his jaws.

When the bear had ambled on up-river, Timpany told me about his life in grizzly country. In his early years he worked as a guide for trophy hunters but tired of the bloodletting and got a job studying chum salmon before moving to Bear Cave Mountain in 1991.

Now in his fifties, having spent more than two thousand days in the company of grizzlies, he has come to know them better than anyone. His relationship with bears is based on mutual respect, exploding the grizzly's fearsome reputation as a natural born killer. 'They are such forgiving animals,' he said. 'When you enter their world you realise what a peaceful coexistence they enjoy.'

As if to prove it, another grizzly materialised from the willow thickets on the opposite bank of the river. This time it was a female known as Mrs Tucker with a yearling cub at her side, close enough for me to hear the crunch of bones as they feasted on a salmon in the shallows.

Her broad back was white with hoar frost and icicles dangled from her belly. 'Hi Mrs Tucker, how're you doing?' said Timpany quietly in his John Wayne drawl as she continued on her way with hardly a glance in our direction. Clearly she was not interested in snacking on a writer long past his sell-by date; not when the river was alive with salmon.

Brian Jackman is a freelance journalist and author with a lifelong passion for travel and wildlife. Today his work appears mostly in *The Daily Telegraph* and *Travel Africa*. Best known as Britain's foremost writer on African wildlife safaris, his African books published by Bradt include *The Marsh Lions* (with Jonathan Scott) and most recently *Savannah Diaries*.

Lion Walking

Joyce West

The stench was unbearable. I stood with a chopper in one hand and a saw in the other. Should I sever the head or leg, or withdraw the entrails? Decisions, decisions.

This was no time for dithering. With the sweltering heat weighing heavily upon me, and the foul odours pervading the air, it was hard to suppress the feeling of nausea rising in my throat. Action was imperative, as the blow flies were hovering in anticipation, and the temperature was soaring.

Surely, in my late seventies I should be engaged in gentler pursuits: a deckchair in my peaceful garden with the perfumes of an English summer wafting on a breeze, an Earl Grey in one hand and a good book in the other, pages rustling as I drifted in and out of my afternoon nap? Instead, I was standing somewhere in the vastness of Africa, feeling very small and insignificant.

I was a volunteer at a lion rehabilitation centre in Zimbabwe. It was run by a third generation white farmer with only one arm, the reason for which was clear. Most of the volunteers were students in their gap year. Obviously I did not come into that category, but the lions were not too particular. I had to participate in whatever work was necessary, because we all worked as a team. No matter how unpleasant the job to be tackled, everyone was expected to do their bit.

The stinking carcass which lay on the ground before me had to be dismembered as quickly as possible into a variety of joints to suit the needs of the eagerly awaiting diners.

When the pile of dismembered cow was ready to be flung into the back of the rusting lorry, we would jump in, joining our bloody load, trying to keep our feet from being completely smothered in intestines as the dilapidated jalopy bumped over the rough terrain. Our destination was one of many enclosures the size of a football pitch for the younger lions. Others were so vast that they disappeared over the distant horizon.

We were driven into these far-flung enclosures at night, with a radio mast held above the lorry, trying to pick up a signal from one of the lions' collars. Some nights we would witness the stalking, ambush and demise of an unfortunate zebra or antelope. Sometimes it was impossible to locate the lions at all.

Before we could feed the waiting lions, we had to entice them into a narrow corridor of their enclosure, where they would be kept until we had deposited the fruits of our morning's labours at the opposite end of the field. The joints and entrails had to be evenly spaced on the ground to lessen the chance of angry fights. We signalled to the keeper waiting by the gate, and he released the hungry lions, who rushed at full speed to leap onto the piles of meat. They growled ferociously throughout their feeding frenzy.

Whilst the minor members of the group devoured their share, one lion – the alpha male, with a flowing black mane and rippling muscles – spread his huge body across his meat, growling menacingly, showing his superiority by eating at his leisure while those of lesser status eyed him warily from a suitable distance.

We would be driven to many more enclosures as there were

ninety-seven lions in total. We needed to feed all of them three times a week. The following day each enclosure had to be cleared of every scrap that had passed through the lions; if anything was left behind, it would soon be covered in flies, maggots and disease, which would mean sick lions. So, on with the large black gloves and the black mask. A group of us volunteers walked in a line a few yards apart across the whole area, picking up faeces, fur, bones and any other nasties and placing them in large bin liners.

Once the cubs reached seventeen months they were mature. Detailed daily data about each lion was recorded then transferred to the computer, which meant that the lions could be assigned to small groups according to their behaviour, strengths and weaknesses. Females live peacefully together in groups of five or six; each group needed several good potential mothers, a few good hunters and, to complete the pride, a healthy male. These would then breed and begin to boost the number of lions. Those new cubs would never have any contact with humans. They would learn their skills from the pride, and eventually be released into the wild. Meanwhile, enclosures fenced with strong wire netting contained the lions, and none of the groups must be in sight of another. Male lions can only live together amicably if no females are close by.

The most important task was to walk every lion under seventeen months old for four hours every day – two hours at dawn and two hours at dusk. This was extremely important as these young lions were all orphans, from various causes. They would have been taught all they needed to know by their parents, but as they had no parents, that was now our task.

We walked in groups of four or five volunteers, with one keeper to three lions. At 6.30 a.m. every day, all volunteers collected a stick.

If the lions ever gave signs that they were about to attack, we held the sticks high above our heads to indicate that we were a bigger pride than them and they would back down. Everyone concentrated on the job, as the lions noticed everything. They would nibble at our ankles as we walked, which was not allowed. We had to smack their cheek, just as their own mother would have done.

When the lions worked out that I was the smallest and weakest in the group, they would give me what is called the 'naughty eye', which was petrifying. Those deep amber eyes would attempt to make eye contact with mine and were frighteningly hypnotic. It was impossible to ignore and I could feel myself being drawn in. With those keen eyes watching me it was hard to appear unafraid and I could sense the hairs on the back of my neck rising. Fortunately, the other volunteers understood what was happening, made a circle around me and raised their sticks. The protection of the weak in the wild is not to be underestimated.

But back to the task at hand. For just a moment or two I paused to take stock of the situation into which I had willingly thrown myself. Then I shook myself into the present, knowing that this was where I had chosen to be. This was the experience of a lifetime and I wasn't going to miss a moment of it. Time to begin! Cow. Chopper. Saw. Stench. Start work!

Following school years in southeast London, which included being evacuated for five years during the war, **Joyce West** spent forty years teaching in primary schools. She married and had two daughters, retired in 1995 and moved to Devon where she became extremely  busy taking 'over-fifties' activity groups, playing tennis and having adventurous holidays.

Parahawking in Nepal

Mary Jean Pramik

When I hit sixty, my eldest daughter said, 'Sixty is the new forty.' These words spawned in me a wanderlust the likes of which I couldn't believe, and weeks after my birthday I challenged myself to go alone to Antarctica. After cavorting with flocks of frenzied penguins and climbing out of a dormant volcano, I returned to Ushuaia in Tierra del Fuego – and an email bearing the news that my ninety-one-year-old father was fading fast. I rushed from Argentina to Ohio to hold his hand for the last five days of his life. I never did tell him, a great watcher of birds, about my adventure with the penguins he would have so loved.

After witnessing his death, I resolved to live more fully in each moment. My happiest twinklings come when I'm somewhere new, moving through uncharted waters. Not only did I commit to hitting the road more frequently each year, I pledged to my father's memory to let go of fears that, at sixty, still held me back.

I have a particular fear of heights. Even Ferris wheels stop me cold. My breath freezes whenever the bucket pauses at the top. I have peered warily at the London Eye, never gathering the gumption to purchase a ticket; similarly, I have always adamantly refused to look down from the Empire State Building, and even when flying I automatically select an aisle seat.

But having watched my father face death with grace and courage, I now vowed to face life without the reticence and trepidation that had tugged at me for a lifetime. It was in this spirit of abandon that I pulled a running jump off the side of Nepal's Sarangkot Mountain at 4,818 feet, parahawking with a bird named Kevin.

❀ ❀ ❀

Before I went to Nepal, the concept of parahawking was entirely foreign to me. The British falconer Scott Mason and his crew created this hybrid of falconry and paragliding in 2001, melding adventure with conservation. The Parahawking Project educates about hawk and vulture flight behaviour and how these birds survive in the wild. Through parahawking tandem rides, the organisation raises funds to restore the nearly decimated vulture population in Nepal.

Vultures have an enduring image problem. People often envision them circling above a nearly dead animal, ready to dive in once it heaves its last breath. On top of humans' general distaste for these creatures, a crisis occurred in the late 1990s when Nepalese, Indian and Pakistani farmers treated their farm animals with the anti-inflammatory diclofenac to reduce their pain as they aged. These creatures eventually died in the open and as the many varieties of Asian vultures rid the streets of the carrion, the diclofenac-laced flesh poisoned the vultures and their numbers decreased precipitously.

Parahawking consists of tandem paragliding while feeding water-buffalo meat to a large raptor. I hung suspended in a bag seat while Scott, a seasoned British paraglider and expert falconer, sat behind me and operated the guide lines and controls. On my maiden flight, I paired with Kevin, a trained white-feathered Egyptian vulture whose black-tipped white wings were a stunning sight to behold, spanning five-and-a-half feet.

Choosing to fly off a cliff was not my usual modus operandi. I had required a slight coaxing. Christina, organiser of my Nepal expedition, had encouraged me. 'They haven't lost anyone yet,' she said. *But there's always a first time*, I thought.

However, my sixty-year-new resolve allowed another rather surprising thought: *If I must die someday, soaring through the unseen wind currents above the white Annapurnas will be as lovely a place as any.*

And in the days leading up to the event I continued trekking the sites around Pokhara, panting my way up to the Shanti Stupa, or Peace Pagoda, the Buddhist shrine on an island in the lake adjoining Pokhara. The stunning view of the Annapurnas kept me in the present.

Kevin is a rescue bird. The Egyptian vulture, which inhabits southern Europe, northern Africa, and western and southern Asia, is one of ten species nearing extinction. On Phewa Lake, Scott's base and home to his young family, Kevin demonstrated his species' expertise at the use of tools by dropping rocks onto an egg to crack the shell. His thin beak and long neck allowed him to claim carrion larger birds cannot.

My only instructions for parahawking were: leap off the cliff and keep running in case the chute doesn't open. *Right*. My mind tried to force my legs to move through the huge and powerful wind gusts. I was slammed back into my harness seat, and a crew member had to help our tandem launch… and then we were off, circling the Sarangkot area with two dozen other paragliders.

In flight, we soared eye-to-eye with the enormous birds, following their movements to catch updrafts and keep our chute apparatus aloft. The eyesight of birds betters that of humans by ten to fifteen times. Their keen eyes identified the swirls of dust defining drafts and currents that were invisible to me on this bright, blue-skied day.

Suspended in the air, time stopped. Scott swooped up, whistling for Kevin. The graceful great vulture made his approach to my outstretched, leather-gloved hand that held his treat. He gently retrieved the fresh-cut water-buffalo chunk that would fuel his long journeys through the air. We repeated this scene many times. I breathed deeply each of the thirty minutes aloft.

One abrupt updraft did surprise me. I had to close my eyes and trust my pilot during a quick right jolt and ascent. We climbed several hundred feet fast, then turned and the entire snow-capped Annapurna range spread out before us.

The sky resplendent with multi-coloured chutes, I found I had no time even to consider my fear. Our half-hour flight ended so gently. Much like Kevin, we glided to a small patch of grass bordering Phewa Lake, smack-dab across the road from the impressive Maya Devi Temple. Enlightenment indeed.

I find myself agreeing more and more with my sometime travelling companion, an Australian septuagenarian whose motto is: 'Comfort travel doesn't interest me.' If anything, I now seek discomfort travel, or travel that offers me opportunities to confront my fears, push my boundaries, expand my worldview and build trust and connections with my fellow creatures on this earth.

I hear some people speak of bucket lists and thousands of places to see before they leave this earth, as if travel exists as a checklist to complete. I find that each second spent travelling breathes life into the following moment of time and place. I now see the distinct shape of each leaf on the trees lining my street and inhale the scent of cantaloupe in my local market with gratitude. I meditate while watching the birds gliding above my San Francisco home. Travelling deepens one's senses and sense of self. It lengthens and stretches out the time we have to challenge ourselves to begin anew, each day to rise above this earth.

Based in California, **Mary Jean (MJ) Pramik** moonlights as a medical writer and contributed to Travelers' Tales *Venturing in...* series on the Canal du Midi, Southern Greece and Ireland, and anthologies on Costa Rica, Bali and Cornwall. She's won Solas Travel Writing awards, and blogs about travel and science at  *Field Notes: Travel in Times of Catastrophic Change* (http://www.mjpramik.com).

Rafting the Barrenlands
Geoff Hinchliffe

We were marooned on a snow-covered sandy ridge in the Barrenlands of Canada's Northwest Territories.

The Twin Otter float plane had dropped us off at the Kathawachaga Lake the previous evening, with all our rafts and supplies for a thirteen-person expedition down the Burnside River. Overnight, the floating ice on the surface had been driven towards us by a change of wind direction, and we were trapped. Unable to launch our rafts, we were forced to appreciate the joys of Arctic camping. A general air of hilarity greeted my announcement that my denture fixative had frozen solid.

We had inflated all three rafts – a real energy-sapping task – and propped them up with the paddles to form windbreaks for the cooking area, then erected our small sleeping tents, and the toilet 'groover' at a suitable distance downwind. All we could do was wait for the ice to retreat.

And wait.

And count how many layers of clothing each of us was wearing. I had seven.

For two days we hiked the surrounding hills; we stalked caribou and Arctic hare; we watched the ice and tested the wind direction; and finally we could launch. Just. After paddling through the floating ice-mush for what seemed like hours on the twisting river, then landing and pitching late camp for the night, we were a mile from where we started, having travelled five shoulder-aching river-miles.

Departure the following morning took us onto the main river and to Nadlock Island in a wide and shallow sweep of the Burnside where the migrating caribou habitually wade and swim, and where Inuit hunters traditionally camped to stock up on meat and hides. As a result, the island has ancient campsites, indicated by the rings of boulders which anchored their hide tents. These tent-rings are filled with hundreds of caribou antlers collected by early archaeologists, and the island is a recognised conservation site, seen by a privileged few. At another ancient Inuit site, our guide Kathy demonstrated the stone kayak racks by sitting on the tundra and paddling an imaginary kayak whilst we stood around admiringly. An observer would have considered us totally mad and they might have been right.

Onwards, onto faster, more exciting waters! During the Arctic winter, deep snow settles on the frozen river until the spring. In the spring thaw, this combined ice and snow breaks into mini-icebergs, beautifully crystalline and far larger than our rafts, making navigation a fraught experience, particularly in the rapids.

Further downstream, we set up camp at Fishing Creek as the sun set gloriously over the tundra, and a wolf watched us from the small hill behind. I felt in need of a clean-up in spite of the bitter wind blowing, and proved myself a mad Englishman to the others with a strip-wash so quickly accomplished it was rudely described as my 'bird bath'.

Bellanca Rapids promised to be a major challenge the next day, with 'boiling' waters to be avoided, in particular where an underwater boulder produces a back-wave or 'stopper' which can easily capsize a raft. We landed upstream for a recce, tossed coins for the order of going, swallowed hard and went for it. Again, the entire procedure was quietly observed by a wolf on the far bank.

Three days followed of relatively gentler progress, allowing us the pleasures of more hikes and wildlife-watching. We were constantly aware of the animal life, but also the birds: golden eagles, rough-legged hawks, peregrine falcons and the semipalmated plover, whose long-legged youngsters ran around the snowbanks. At one point we stopped opposite a high river cliff, and a nesting pair of gyrfalcons objected with screeches to our presence. On a hike up a side stream we happened on a family of musk oxen, a survival from the Stone Age, which to our delight did not stampede but posed for photographs on the opposite bank. The Arctic plant life, close to the ground as it is, was also utterly absorbing. Wherever I looked there were louseworts, arnica, wild wallflowers, poppies, saxifrages, lupins, vetch, fireweed, blueberry, bearberry, ground-hugging willow trees only inches high and, of course, eye-catching lichens on every rock.

A two-day camp coincidentally covered my sixty-second birthday. Until then I had been unaware that the supplies included a large cupcake with two candles, especially secreted away for my birthday; the other sixty candles had to wait until we got back, I was told. The following day was Canada Day, so we rigged up the camp shower and took turns to wash, before letting off a celebratory flare after dinner as a substitute fireworks display. Not long after, we crossed the Arctic Circle, and everybody wanted a picture for their albums. We all posed with the circular rim of a bailing bucket, feeling like nutters.

There was another magic moment when a wolverine appeared on the river bank. We couldn't stop to watch, as rafts don't have brakes.

Wolverines – giant members of the weasel family – are so rare that some Inuit have never seen one. Yet within an hour we spotted another, and soon after a mother grizzly lolloped across a hillside snowbank with her cub in close attendance. This time, we were glad not to stop. Our campsite that night was invaded by two musk oxen during supper, and we visited the den of an Arctic fox. The following morning we drifted beneath the nesting ledge of a pair of peregrine falcons.

A peaceful paddling day took us to our final campsite, about two miles above Burnside Falls. We enjoyed another wilderness sunset evening and after finishing off all the food rations except the following morning's breakfast, we slept rather well. The rafts had done their job.

In the morning we deflated the rafts and packed up before one final hike to the head of the falls. The plane was scheduled to collect us later. The Twin Otter, this time on wheels with a bush pilot, would land on the very short hilltop and take me and the gear to Bathurst, then return to fly everybody else to Yellowknife. That was the plan.

Then bad weather set in.

Mike, the pilot, couldn't spot us.

We had to reinflate a raft just for shelter on the open hilltop.

Three shivering hours later, Mike radioed to say that he'd have a go at landing. Twice he roared over, seemingly parting our hair, before landing in a flurry of rain, muck and reverse thrust. We duly loaded up all the gear, leaving the accumulated toilet groovers (like rather unsavoury dustbins) until the end. It was my job, wedged in amongst them, to keep them upright.

Mike taxied the plane to the farthest back edge of the hilltop, revved the engines, released the brakes, and across the ground we bounced and bucketed. The edge came nearer, and nearer.

We reached the end of the hill and fell off it into space, dropping over two hundred feet before going into level flight above the river.

'Just as expected,' Mike said later, somewhat nonchalantly. And there I was, nursing the 'groover' buckets. It seemed a pity they were unavailable.

Geoff Hinchliffe is a retired maths teacher who considers himself lucky to have been able to travel quite extensively into the world's empty spaces, including both polar regions, and particularly Canada's Northwest Territories and Nunavut, where he had this adventure.

My Creaking Bones

Debbie Parrott

A snorting, grunting growl rumbled over the crest of the kopje. My eyes snapped open.

What was it?

Hyena or lion?

Near or far?

Our armed Maasai guard was motionless and apparently asleep. Then, blushing into the night, I realised where the noise had come from.

I'd been snoring.

I wriggled uncomfortably, eased my arms out of the sleeping bag and tip-toed stiff fingers along the rock beneath me. It was unbelievable; I was lying fifty metres above the plains on a huge, isolated outcrop of granite.

How had that happened – at my age?

'It'll be fun,' Annie had said. 'We'll have supper as the sun goes down, breakfast as it rises, the boys will bring the horses out in the morning and we can ride back to the lodge. Are you up for it?'

I was... but would someone speak to my body?

The night sky was wrapping itself loosely round the curve of the earth. I tried to pick out patterns amidst the jostling stars but I couldn't isolate a single constellation; it was a celestial mess. When

I was home, and the grandchildren were taunting me with their youth, I would conjure this memory and be smug.

With hips groaning against the granite beneath, I waited for sleep. By dawn, I was dozing, curled up and snug, when the birds began to sing and squawk. Twittering arias floated up from the savanna as they bombarded the riot of insects. I was too high up to see them but I knew they would be swooping and darting. I unfurled slowly like an ancient scroll; the sky burned an intense orange as the sun announced her imminent arrival and garish brushstrokes of vivid pink swept the horizon.

'Cup of tea, Debbie?'

Annie sat down beside me and we stared at the paint palette until it dissolved and the sun took control of the day. Obediently, the sky turned a forget-me-not blue.

Looking east I could see the snaking cinder cones of the Chyulu Hills in the distance. I knew ol Donyo Lodge was there but it had been built to blend and it was pressed, chameleon like, into the volcanic hillside. From my room at the lodge, the huge kopje that I had just spent the night on looked like a distant and isolated wart.

Annie was gingerly poking branches in the fire.

'Sorry, this is on its last gasp, it won't make breakfast but it'll do another cuppa.' She lifted the elephantine kettle and poured. I clutched the mug and the warmth eased my knuckles into the day. Looking west, Mount Kilimanjaro rose majestically a mere sixty miles away, her foothills in neighbouring Tanzania. The snow crept down from the summit like icing on a bun. Sitting atop my own personal monolith I felt, at the very least, equal to the majesty before me.

'Come on Debbie, I can see them coming.' She shaded her eyes with a hand and pointed, 'Over there.'

I followed her finger and could see puffs of dust clouds billowing behind ant-sized horses. The 'kopje housekeeping' had already arrived in the form of a Land Rover and two Maasai staff from the lodge. I watched the latter scrambling up and down the rocks and reflected on their concern the night before as they had witnessed my ascent. They had obviously assumed I had 'a goat loose in the *shamba*' as I proceeded mainly on all fours and, on one occasion, slug-like after traversing a chasm while muttering repeatedly, 'I think I can, I know I can.'

As for the descent, I simply pictured my two-year-old grandson bouncing down the stairs…

The horses and guides arrived, along with the next challenge of the day: mounting.

'*Habari ya asubuhi!*' shouted Paul. 'Good morning! The horses are a little jumpy; we have just disturbed some lion.'

A lead ball set off at a gentle roll around my stomach.

I was potentially riding the main course for a leonine lunch, while offering myself as dessert. It wasn't a thought that filled me with confidence.

As if reading my mind, Paul said, 'A baby giraffe will make a better meal for a lion than you. You'd be a bit scrawny and tough!'

He laughed and his teeth were like white doors in moonlight.

'Are we going back the same way?' I asked tentatively.

'We go that way.' Paul waved an arm airily in no particular direction, then added, 'If they attack they will go for the horse at the back but they had full stomachs so it shouldn't be a problem.'

The large rock we found was not quite fit for purpose but a useful aid and, with a bit of Maasai heavy-handedness, I was spooned into the saddle.

I swallowed nervously – and rode at the front.

We weaved along a flattened, grassy path. The savanna stretched to its inevitable collision with the horizon.

'Ready to trot, then canter?' called Paul.

'Ready!' And showing off, I added, '*Twende, twende,*' – Swahili for 'Let's go.'

The sun warmed my bones and they softened into the canter. We left the track to head across the plains; the horses loved it and the riders loved it. Looking out for holes created by the savanna night-shift, we rushed on, fanning out to find our own pockets of freedom. I was twenty-one again!

A family of warthogs broke cover and ran for it, their tails held aloft like aerials on remote control cars, the youngsters barely visible above the seed heads apart from ears and tail tips. The plains were studded with umbrella acacia trees, their parasol branches spreading to create much needed shade. As we got closer to the lodge and the trees became denser, I scanned the half-light under leafy canopies for flicking ears and amber eyes.

Giraffes were everywhere, their heads poking up like periscopes. They had thick blue tongues to cope with the vicious acacia thorns and when we strolled past barely metres away from them on horseback, they merely fluttered long lashes at us. Occasionally, if we surprised them, they would burst into life and gallop off; left legs then right legs, their necks acting as balancing joysticks.

The horses picked their way through scrubby thicket, stepping neatly over stones and cracking twigs underfoot. Then a large crack came. Then again. Snap! Crackle! Rustle!

Paul whispered, 'Can you see it yet?'

See what? I thought, eyes straining. Acacia, a few large boulders, logs, bushes... Nothing. Then a 'boulder' started to tremble; with a furious flapping of ears and an irritated shaking of its head, an elephant trampled towards us flashing long, curving tusks. I shrank into the saddle. My horse shifted nervously beneath me. We turned and walked slowly away, resisting the violent urge to charge off in a choking dust storm. Fortunately, the elephant was only disgruntled at having his privacy disturbed and he stomped off like a teenager (which he probably was) to address the needs of his stomach rather than his territory – we had merely caught him unawares.

'What would we have done if he had charged us?' I asked Paul.

A smile spread across his face. 'We would have galloped away. It would have been fun!'

Would it? I thought.

We meandered among trees until we came to a soft track of lava ash, then we cantered on, surprising a small herd of impala that scattered before us like escaping fire sparks.

Rounding a bend, Paul stopped suddenly, and we concertinaed behind him. 'Leopard!'

I stopped. Beneath the stillness a frenzy of heartbeats clattered. Paul stood up in his stirrups and peered into the scrub.

An ambush?

I followed his stare and out from the bush waddled a beautiful leopard... tortoise. Sensing us there, it retracted its legs, pulled in its head and plopped to the ground. The sun glistened on its puckered, checkerboard shell; it was a rare and lucky sighting.

'You wouldn't have seen that in a car,' observed Paul.

Or the pair of black-backed jackals we had seen the day before; the little creatures had paced along beside us as if it was part of their daily routine. The horses had not taken the slightest notice of them.

The lodge could now be seen in the contours of the hill, as if it had grown there from a seed. The horses, sensing breakfast and a loosening of girths, instinctively popped a little bounce into their pace.

With the stables in sight, and while congratulating myself on a lion-free ride, I carelessly destroyed hours of meticulous work. A slender thread draped over my riding hat and from the remnants of a spider's web clinging precariously to the branch of a tree, a magnificent golden orb spider glared out at me. I was slightly mollified to see that she had not lost her pantry; a long line dangled, swinging gently in the breeze with an assortment of insects still firmly glued to it. At least she wouldn't go hungry as she set about rebuilding.

We walked on with long reins into the yard and the grooms came to greet us.

'Good ride? Good ride?'

'Good night? You sleep well?'

'Did you see lion?'

'Did Mawingu canter well for you?'

Questions bounced around the yard as the stable boys practised their English.

'Breathtaking! Amazing! Fantastic,' I fired back.

All I had to do now was dismount, not my most flattering manoeuvre, swallow a couple of anti-inflammatories and stagger to a hot bath.

That evening, overlooking the plains, with a 'medicinal' dawa cocktail of vodka, ice, honey and mint, I wondered if death on a Kenyan plain might be considerably better than withering away in a high-backed chair at some random home for the elderly... I had another dawa and toasted myself.

Debbie Parrott from Guernsey in the Channel Islands has travelled all her life, starting with family camping holidays throughout Europe and progressing to worldwide travel. Only recently has she started to write articles based on her many travel diaries. Apart from the local Eisteddfod, this is her first competition entry.

A Meeting with Ganesh
Penny Turner

Let a person walk alone with few wishes, committing no wrong, like an elephant in the forest.
The Dhammapada, *Chapter 23, The Elephant*

We lay in the undergrowth. Kate had a slightly bemused look on her face. I probably did too.

Question: Why were we – two sixty-something women – lying under lantana bushes in an Indian forest, hardly daring to breathe because of the noise the dried leaves made as our ribs moved?

Answer: We were hiding from elephants.

We had set off early in the morning for our jungle trek. Our guide, Y (he wants to remain anonymous), assured us that we were most unlikely to meet wild elephants. However, before he let us start, he made it clear that if the worst happened and we did encounter elephants, there were safety precautions that we must agree to undertake without question. I'm ashamed to say we listened to the instructions with a certain amount of scepticism. Our eyes glazed over as we politely gave the impression of paying attention. We promised to obey orders, because Y made it clear we wouldn't be going on a walk if we didn't. We thought Y was hyping up the danger to give us old dears a thrilling story to take home.

We walked through gorgeous forest by the fabulously beautiful Cauvery River and were told all kinds of interesting facts about the wildlife that so abundantly surrounded us. We indignantly rejected the five-kilometre walk that Y considerately suggested was less tiring for oldies like us in favour of the eight-kilometre one.

A bad decision: after about half an hour of dithering about looking at nature and being overwhelmed by beauty and so on, we noticed that Y had stopped talking and seemed frozen to the spot.

He had smelled elephants, and ordered a frantic dash for cover. He was totally silent as he moved and was deeply dismayed by our thunderous racket as we did our best to run quietly after him.

Y left us hidden in the undergrowth (which suddenly seemed very flimsy), and crept off to locate the elephants more precisely so he could work out what they were going to do next and so plan our escape.

Some time later, a slight rustling in the lantana alerted us to his return. The fact that he was shaking and smelt of the acrid sweat that only real fear provokes told us our situation wasn't good.

'Roll,' he gasped. 'Roll to where I am.'

Kate was the first to go. Holding her camera high in the air she rolled competently towards the deep undergrowth that Y had indicated.

Then I rolled. I rolled onto my camera and then onto my binoculars, which caused a change of direction so I landed on a small lantana sapling where I got stuck. I started to giggle helplessly. It was only Y's agonised gesturing that got me to pull myself together. I can't guess how long the three of us lay there nose-down in the leaf mould: they don't do that kind of time in watches, as they say.

When the sound of the giant bamboo being smashed and

trampled by feeding elephants grew faint and the frightening stench of elephant became less pervasive, Y murmured that he was off again to reconnoitre.

After a longish time he was back.

'They're moving away,' he whispered. 'We've gotta get out of here NOW!'

He didn't want us all to go together, because bitter experience had taught him about the astounding noise we could make. So he grasped my hand (he obviously thought that Kate, unlike me, would behave sensibly if left unsupervised) and dragged me along a narrow path. I crashed and stumbled through dead leaves and fallen branches. Y left me cowering under yet more lantana, and went back for Kate. I soon heard her puffing and stamping through the leaves just as embarrassingly loudly as I had done.

Y felt it was now safe to move on together. 'My prayers were answered,' he blurted. 'I found the courage not to abandon you to the elephants.'

Half an hour later we reached a tribal village. A villager shouted something urgently.

'What did he say?'

'There's a bad elephant in the forest, so don't go there.'

As soon as he had delivered us safely home, Y made his excuses and left. He probably, and understandably, had an overpowering need to be somewhere completely free of clumsy, aged English women.

Kate and I sat in the shady dining room above the lovely, sacred Cauvery River. Kate sucked at a large beer. I drank coffee. We looked upstream towards the scene of our adventure. Our eyes met. I gave a snort of mirth.

Question: Why were we – two sixtyish women, one of whom had

shot coffee down her nostrils and all over the table cloth – howling with laughter in an elegant dining room beside the holy river in Karnataka province, India?

Answer: Because (as we knew, having visited an ancient Buddhist temple and then read up a bit) the Buddha teaches:

'When you realise how perfect everything is you will tilt your head back and laugh at the sky.'

Penny Turner has lived in Greece for many years and has worked for most of the environmental NGOs there; she spent eleven years travelling through the wildest parts with her horse, George. A Fellow of the Royal Geographical Society and a member of the Long Riders Guild, she currently teaches English in Krakow, Poland.

Risks, Scrapes and Strange Journeys

The Last Stronghold
Colin Thubron

In his sixties, Colin Thubron traced the first great trade route out of China into the mountains of Central Asia, across northern Afghanistan and the plains of Iran into Kurdish Turkey, covering seven thousand miles in eight months on buses, donkey carts, trains and camels. Here he finds the last stronghold of the Assassin sect, besieged by the Mongol army in 1256. The last Grand Master of the sect, Rukn-ad-din, had walled himself up in his cliff-castle before eventually surrendering, but the castle was put to the torch. Thubron looks for men with climbing equipment but one is absent and the other says it is too dangerous.

Dawn broke softly over the mountain. In the cleaned light, far beyond the orchards and poplars of Shams Kilaya, the castle precipice lifted two thousand feet above the valley floor in wrinkles of pink stone. Dogs were emptying garbage-cans in the street as I left. The air was cold. I went through cherry orchards, picking at ripe blackberries, while the rose-coloured bluff grew in front. Beyond a thin stream the slopes were furred in grass and climbed past a small shrine into wilderness.

Now the whole mountain spread above me. It was split by clefts which ate their way up half its height, then delved into artificial-looking caves. Scree and boulders loosened and cascaded under my feet. In the airy silence their brittle grating was the only sound, like pebbles dragged by the tide. Nothing moved in the stone valley. It was as if the stream below marked a divide between the present and a shunned past. I followed a goat-track along the foot of the bluffs. I had imagined them untouched: but now, vertically above me, I made out scarps which had once been plastered, and the swell of a round tower. In the southwest angle, a change of light awoke walls reaching sixty feet up – a coating of brick stuccoed hard against the cliff, almost indistinguishable from it. Diagonal seams of rock might once have been stairways. The crescent of an arch showed clear in a cave, where swallows were flying in and out. The whole mountain was one vast, riddled sanctuary.

I longed to enter. But the cavern-mouths gaped sixty feet sheer above, blackened where fire had raged inside, their outer structures burnt away. When I scrutinised the fissures ascending to them, only one seemed to offer a few thin holds. Tentatively at first, I started to climb its crevice. But under my fingers the solid-looking cliff felt loose and friable, and I realised that the whole mountain – perhaps the stark crags of all this region – was not living rock but a coagulate of sand and shale.

At first my body seemed light to me, and swung easily into the spaces I planned for it. I was a little surprised. When I tested the soft-looking scarp, kicking or wrenching at it before each step, nothing crumbled. My trainers felt out invisible knobs and dents. Slowly, clambering from side to side, I was winching myself into space. Then stones began to skitter down below me, and echoed on the rocks. A sharp wind was blowing over the higher cliffs. Little by little, I became afraid. I had not really thought the ascent possible.

Halfway up, my nerve failed me. I stopped, spread-eagled against the rock-face. A few drops of rain fell. Above me the crevice – thirty feet of it – rose sheer. Beneath me was a drop to solid stone. I could see the autumn valley descending past the oasis of Shams Kilaya to hills like grey dust. I waited for my breathing to still. I noticed the hands clenching the rock close against my face: they were lean and broken-skinned, not hands that should be doing this. Then I looked up and glimpsed the ceiling of the cave-chamber I could not reach. It was sooted by Mongol fires.

With helpless excitement I began to crawl upwards again. It became too late to turn back. Years ago, young, I would have hurried in fear and perhaps fallen. Now I waited, with pained slowness, to secure a handhold here, a foothold there. I could hear my own heart. For the last ten feet the sides of the cleft were so close that I braced my body inside it. Once I felt my toes slipping; then they held. I was afraid to look down. A broken arch appeared in the opening above. The scarp beside me had been cemented smooth.

Only when I heaved myself on to the level floor, heady with triumph, did I look down at the sixty-foot drop to stone, shaking with the thought of my descent. I was in a huge broken chamber. Outside, but close by, the hewn stone of a tower bulged from the plaster.

❖ ❖ ❖

Now I can barely read what I wrote there. In my notebook half the sentences tremble indecipherably. But I think they say this:

I do not know where I am. In stables, maybe, or a guardhouse. An arch spans the cleft where a bastion once stood. Whatever passageway it connected has fallen in. A room has broken open above it. I am treading lightly, for fear of falling. All the ceilings are charred.

Somewhere I remember smoothing my hands over a long, mortared cistern. Beyond, I grope down a rough-hewn corridor fifty yards into the mountain, until it opens on a high vault. I have no torch, and cannot go farther. I sit down exhausted in the opening above the valley, gazing at the traces of stucco flaking round its threshold. I feel light and strange. The soot-stains are still vivid there. I think of Rukn-ad-din and his family hurrying down these passageways to some lost stairway, going to their surrender and to death. I steady my nerves for my own descent. Birds flitter and squeak in the fissures, and an invisible sun is shining out of storm-clouds over other mountains.

Colin Thubron is an award-winning master of travel writing and novelist. His first books were about the Middle East – Damascus, Lebanon and Cyprus. In 1982 he travelled in the Soviet Union, pursued by the KGB. These early experiences were followed by his best-known travel  books: on China, Central Asia and Siberia, including *Shadow of the Silk Road*. He lives in London.

The above passage is reprinted from *Shadow of the Silk Road*, by kind permission. © Colin Thubron 2006

On a Road to Italy

Elizabeth Pimm

Shall I paint
  Or write a book
Lay (on) tiled floors
Or have a look at
Where I fit into a world
That's less prescribed
Where mornings come
And evenings go
And no-one really has to know
Just where I am
Or what I do
Just me to say
What kind of day

We planned to retire in Italy. I had said 'yes' on the Ponte Vecchio in Florence (for a nervous second time but I couldn't really say no in that setting, could I?) and we spent a stunning week in a villa near the 'town of fine towers', San Gimignano, exploring Tuscany.

Oh my! We later fell out spectacularly and I wondered what was left of me and my life.

There is always more, so one weekend on the spur of the moment I booked a '1p' flight with a well-known airline, took a bus from Ancona to Macerata, an opera centre, and fell completely in love with Le Marche. Two years later I had retired and restored a derelict farmhouse with the help of a larger-than-life geometer who also liked opera. When friends came to celebrate completion, he brought his wife and daughter to lunch and his mistress to dinner. Life was interesting again.

It was so much easier to bring what I needed for my house in the car. I had driven to Italy on my own before and started off again. I remember a beautiful day and a conscious feeling of well-being. It was past lunchtime as I approached Saint-Quentin in northern France so I filled up with petrol, parked the car and joined the many travellers at a café. Feeling suitably refreshed after a quiche and coffee, I set off enthusiastically for Colmar, my usual stop for the night. Colmar being on the Alsace wine route, I looked forward to a cool glass of Gewurztraminer with blue cheese when I arrived – a delicious combination and a great pick-me-up after a long day's drive.

I was soon in the fast lane when – bang! – a tyre blew and I briefly lost control of the steering. Thank God I was able to cross lanes without mishap, coming to a shaky stop on the verge. I hardly had time to register what had happened when a car stopped ahead of me and a young man offered his assistance. We unpacked the boot to find the safety triangle and the spare wheel.

'I don't really know how to change a wheel,' he said. 'I'll get my friend to help.' He hurried off – and they drove away.

Ah well, I thought, I'll have to do it myself.

But all was gone. His accomplice had taken my large handbag with purse, cards, keys, mobile phones, sunglasses, passport, Italian identity card and residence permit, leather jacket and even the maps. Not possible! I was shaking before. Now I was stunned.

The car swayed each time another car sped past. Would anyone stop, and did I really want them to?

I felt unbelievably vulnerable without any of the essentials we normally take for granted.

A woman swerved in, paused and said she would notify the police. The two gendarmes were annoyed. Why was I so stupid as to travel alone on the motorway? These foreigners score your tyre, follow you until it blows and then offer to help. If I had realised what they were up to I would probably have been knifed.

I wondered who 'these foreigners' were. I gathered they were recent immigrants. It is so easy to blame others.

The gendarmes put on the temporary wheel and I followed them to their offices, where they said I couldn't use their phone to cancel my cards or phones (a VERY expensive delay) as they needed them for emergencies. Since I had no money, they escorted me to a cheap hostel mainly occupied by 'these foreigners'.

Were they there, and could things get any worse?

The receptionist allowed me to call my partner. Could I quote his card number and details to pay just for this hostel and to get a new tyre on Monday morning? It was Saturday afternoon. I finished my book and a large collection of Sudoku puzzles and found two hundred euros in my suitcase which might be just enough to get me to my destination. I felt hungry, frightened and lost. A former Italian neighbour had once said, *Sia risoluta*, 'be resolute', and a Frenchman in another sticky situation advised, '*Courage, Madame*.' Now was the time.

The receptionist gave me an enormous cheese baguette for

Sunday lunch. I loved her! With my partner's card details, I talked my way into a new wheel at opening time on Monday and carried on. Having previously stayed in the hotel I had booked in Colmar they agreed to let me eat, stay and pay on my return journey. There is a lot of kindness out there too!

Would the petrol run out before I reached the farmhouse? I stumbled in late at night, running on empty, and my new house enveloped me, helping to restore some equilibrium.

Over the next few days I laid a stone path to dissipate some of my nervous energy, ate delicious pasta (I had some money in Italy), turned the music up to full blast and thanked my lucky, and very beautiful, stars as I looked over the soft hills in the evening.

Dispersed

Black bug crawls slowly over tiles
Mozart clear in the enormous stillness
Windows look on pale enveloping grey
Fields fallow, leaves still
An autumn day
The sounds demand attention
Breaking through black crawling thoughts
Order, melody and grace impinge
Not as background but pulling towards immediacy
Two hundred years of notes reaching the now of aloneness
Giving beauty, soul and new cadence
From timeless expression

Although not ready I drove myself back, hardly daring to let the car out of my sight. I was allowed back into England without a passport, or anything else. I probably looked shattered enough to be believed, and burst into floods of relieved tears when I reached Cambridge.

Ongoing oldies are crazy! I made a point of driving out to Italy again on my own a short while later, taking picnic sandwiches and a large flask of strong coffee. No need for motorway services this time.

There's no stopping us.

Educated in India, England, Ireland and Australia, **Elizabeth Pimm** worked in Radio Astronomy and Vision Research before studying Optometry and running her practice in Cambridge. On retirement she invented a baby  product and restored an Italian farm. She has two children and three brilliant grandchildren. She writes for pleasure and sanity.

Gently Down the Stream
John Carter

B efore inviting you to travel with me from this opening sentence to the end of my tale, I have a confession to make.

Don't be too concerned, I haven't committed a really big crime of the kind that is admitted at the end of TV detective programme – when all the participants are gathered in the drawing room, and shortly after one of them says: 'Good grief, Inspector, you don't mean to say the murderer is *one of us?*' No, nothing like that at all.

My confession is that I have forgotten some of the details. I can recall most of the basics, and can assure you that the story is true, but I can't recall exactly when it happened or the names of all the people who were there at the time.

I know we were in Switzerland, and I think it might have been 1995 or 1996 – a long time ago, I admit, but, though I may not yet have qualified for a free TV licence, I was well within free bus-pass territory.

We were making a destination report for a TV travel show. Doug was there, directing our team effort – I know that for a fact, because I confirmed it with him just a few days ago – and I am pretty sure the lovely Kim was our production assistant. It is the names of cameraman, assistant cameraman and sound recordist which escape me.

Would you mind awfully if I call them Tom, Dick and Harry?

I'm also not exactly sure which particular bit of Switzerland we were in. I seem to recall going on a train that went up *inside* a mountain, the Jungfraujoch.

At the end of the line we got off the train – still inside the mountain – and entered something called the Ice Palace, located inside a glacier.

The first thing I saw was a trio of Japanese ladies in traditional kimonos having their picture taken, giggling and shivering at the same time as they stood before a larger-than-life-size statue of Sherlock Holmes, carved in ice.

The Mikado meets *The Hound of the Baskervilles*. And very surreal.

But I digress. Let's get back to the basics of my tale.

It began much the same as most working trips began. A brief as to the kind of story we were looking for, some research before departure and then a flight out to start gathering relevant images and sound, a few interviews if necessary and two or three pithy pieces to camera by yours truly.

It was the type of story I had produced many times, a visit to a region better known for its winter attractions to see what it offered in the summer – a season when cable cars whisked visitors up to walking rather than skiing terrain: when the older and less agile wandered through flower-strewn meadows, tackling the gentlest of slopes on their way to a nice cream tea in a picturesque village.

We'd lay melodies from *The Sound of Music* over most of the long shots (I know it's not the correct country, but the sentiment's the same), and make sure Harry recorded plenty of cowbells. Should we encounter any happy ramblers in the right age bracket I would infiltrate their ranks and maybe even interview some of them.

Tom and Dick would be more than happy, as the scenery would be spectacular and they could indulge in the long, slow panning shots that cameramen love – and which, incidentally, were a boon to those of us who wrote our own commentaries (and not everybody did, but that's another story).

As I say, it was all straightforward and predictable. Or so I thought.

For reasons which escape me to this day, Doug decided to broaden the scope of the report to include sequences that would appeal to our younger and more active viewers. I wasn't especially pleased about this, as the things he had in mind could cause harm to an old duffer like me. Mountain biking, for example.

We compromised on the mountain biking. The liaison lady from the local tourist office rounded up some suitable lads and lassies. Tom and Dick filmed them travelling at high speed downhill, on rough tracks through trees. And I added a few words, off screen, along the lines of 'and for those who want something a little livelier, this should provide the thrills…'

There was talk of rock climbing, too. Having brought no equipment with me (who would?) I managed to wheedle my way out of that. We took some suitable pictures, I said something – again, off screen – about having a head for heights, and that was that.

Now I don't want you to think I am not up for anything adventurous or even hazardous. From my earliest days as a travel writer and reporter, I have been prepared to give things a go, especially during the thirty years of my television travel career.

In those long-ago days before the camera drone was invented, the only way to get aerial shots was to hire a helicopter. And the first thing we did with it was take the door off so the cameraman could work unimpeded. Most of the helicopters I have flown in have been doorless. There was no other way to do it, though it carried an element of risk.

Similarly, when required to do so, I ran with the bulls at Pamplona – every morning for a week – though I was much younger then, and I have to admit that alcohol played its part. So I am no coward. However, with age comes caution.

After four days in Switzerland, and just when I thought I was going to complete this assignment in one piece, Doug came up with his masterstroke.

'Whitewater rafting,' he said one evening, towards the end of a very decent and quite well-lubricated dinner. 'I hear you can go whitewater rafting in this area.'

The liaison lady, also reasonably well-lubricated, said it would be no problem to get that organised for us. Which, next morning, she proceeded to do.

Thus it came to pass that we assembled in the lobby of our hotel to meet half a dozen young locals who were to take us on our little adventure. They were impressive, being all very tall and unbelievably fit. In winter they were ski instructors, and during the rest of the year switched to being mountaineers. If I had to go whitewater rafting with anyone, these lads were ideal companions. However, I hoped it wouldn't come to that, as I had a little plan.

We squeezed into wetsuits, then squeezed into a couple of long-wheelbase Land Rovers to drive to our starting point. En route we dropped off cameraman Tom at a high point overlooking the river, from which he could film us passing. Assistant Dick, with a smaller, waterproof, camera, would join Doug and me in the large rubber inflatable boat, moored and waiting for us a few miles upstream.

When we got there, Harry, declaring firmly that 'You won't need location sound for this,' remained in the Land Rover.

As we clambered from bank to boat, I mentioned that I couldn't swim. Would this be a problem?

Instead of saying that it would, and I would have to stay behind, one of the lads replied that if the boat capsized we should lie back on the water and let the current take us feet first.

Swimming was not an option in such fast-flowing water. (He didn't mention, until long afterwards, that swimming wouldn't help, as we would be instantly dashed to our deaths against the rocks.)

So my plan had come to naught. The river was extremely fast and foamy. I don't know if 'foamy' is a proper word, but that's what it was. Extremely foamy. And bubbly and, when it wasn't foamy and bubbly, clear and green. And dangerous.

It rushed and roared beyond control between steep banks, as the melting snows of spring swelled its course. It tumbled and twisted past great smooth rocks, black and brown and all too obviously lethal. But there was no turning back as we climbed into the boat.

We settled ourselves in. And cast off.

Within seconds the boat was travelling at high speed between the rocks, bouncing and bobbing and taking us where it willed, despite the efforts of the lads to steer it away from the worst of the dangers. I clung to the ropes attached to the rounded sides of our craft, loudly blaspheming and praying in equal measure.

After what seemed like an hour – in reality about fifteen minutes – the river calmed down and we drifted to the shore where the Land Rovers, having raced down the road, were waiting for us.

On the bank, trembling and dripping, I heard Dick say his waterproof camera had proved to be nothing of the sort, so there would be hardly anything worth using from him. Tom chimed in with the comment that, having filmed us passing, he had, on the way down, spotted an even better vantage point from which he could get some sensational shots to make up for the lack of footage from Dick. However, this required us to do the whole thing again.

And we did. Don't ask. I don't want to think about it.

Eventually we made it back to our hotel, stripped off our wetsuits and joined the lads in the bar for restorative brandies.

'You did very well, for a man of your years,' one of them said, towering over me and waving his brandy glass in an expansive fashion. I was about to make an appropriately barbed response when I realised I was not merely old enough to be his father, but pretty close to being the same age as his grandfather.

So I said: 'Well, you obviously knew what you were doing, so I felt quite confident. Incidentally, how many times have you made that run?'

'Including the two runs today?' he asked.

'Including the two runs today,' I replied.

'Three times.'

'*Three times?!*' I stared in disbelief. '*Only three bloody times?!*'

And then the truth was reluctantly revealed. The liaison lady hadn't wanted to let us down, so she had asked her chums to obtain a rubber boat, find a stretch of fast river and take us down it.

Only the previous day they had tried out that particular stretch of that particular river and, having somehow survived, decided it would do. They didn't usually do whitewater rafting, being too busy being ski instructors or climbing mountains, but hadn't wanted to disappoint us.

People used to tell me, 'Honestly, what a job. Life's one long holiday for you.'

Yeah. Right.

Appointed Travel Correspondent by *The Times* in 1967 (the first in the paper's history), **John Carter** combined the role with that of reporter/presenter on BBC TV's *Holiday* programme – a series he helped create – from 1969 until 1987, when he moved to ITV's *Wish You Were Here...?* He also broadcast  regularly on Radio 4's Jimmy Young Programme. He continues to travel and write, but for pleasure not profit. He is currently compiling an anthology of traveller's tales – all true, mostly unbelievable – to be published in due course by Bradt.

Relic of the Raj

Jane Wilson-Howarth

We'd risen before dawn. Sulphurous air hung thick, warm and misty. We negotiated cracked paving stones over odiferous storm drains, splats of red betel spit and razor wire protruding from buildings. Someone had nailed a tiny spirit house to a banyan tree. A crazy koel call came from a cuckoo. Crows shouted surprised *aggh, agghs*.

South Asia is in my bones. I met my husband there; my children were conceived and spent their early years there. My middle son is buried there. But this was a new country for me, a troubled country where everyone stared but everyone smiled and people put themselves out for outsiders. The sounds, spicy smells and *paan*-sellers reminded me of scenes I'd experienced in 1976, the first time I visited India at the tender age of twenty-two. This was no surprise as Burma had been part of British India for sixty-two years, and large numbers of Indians moved in to take administrative jobs for the Raj. Yet local manners, gracefulness and roadside shrines also recalled destinations further east, in Thailand and Indonesia. I felt I was visiting a cultural crossroads: the bridge between south and southeast Asia.

Yangon Central Station was seething with families and impossible amounts of luggage yet it was surprisingly quiet. Neon lights shone harshly. Three-metre-high railings stopped anyone getting close to the trains. I found a seat, grateful to rest my aching knees, and waited, watching small children in their best going-out clothes playing tag amidst the packages and cases. I hoped we were in the right place. It was hard to tell; we'd been rendered illiterate, unable even to read numbers.

There was simply nothing recognisable in the Myanmar language, a script that although based on Sanskrit has so evolved that we could identify very few letters. Most were circles with various pieces missing or twiddly bits added. This had made even buying our tickets challenging. A couple of days earlier we'd gone to the station, intent on taking the night train to Mandalay. The ticket office was closed and clearly hadn't been functional for years. Someone official-looking directed us over the railway line. On that side there was nothing that seemed remotely like the kind of place you'd buy a ticket. Another official pointed us out of the station to a different building. Knowing that the grand colonial railway offices were being converted into a hotel, we had very little idea where to go next, but then down an alley I spotted a shed with corrugated iron for a roof. It looked like a place cattle might be auctioned. It didn't have many walls. Inside there were rows of ticket counters. The lack of walls let the air move so it was a little cooler inside. Chirpy tree sparrows were enjoying the echoes that they could make. The only sign in English said 'Complaint Centre'; it alluded to a small red post box, definitely a relic of the Raj. A couple of counters were manned so we approached one and the official asked whether we would travel Ordinary or Upper Class. We wanted Upper Class. He pointed behind us to another set of counters and told us we needed number two.

The counters were labelled in Myanmar only but we plumped for the second counter from the left. It was unmanned. Simon made the bold move of putting his head into the office to ask for a ticket on the night train. We needed counter six. The man there established that the night train was fully booked for the next couple of nights. I wondered whether this was the time to offer a bribe, but didn't. Simon asked for a ticket to travel during the day, but for that we were assured we needed to return to the railway station.

We doubted that was true. A koel joined the negotiations, shouting increasingly manically so it sounded as if the heat had completely fried its brain. We were not yet frazzled. It was early. We had time and explained we wanted to travel the day after tomorrow. We were directed to counter five. The man at counter five directed us to counter seven and someone else to counter eight. The official at counter eight needed to see our passports. We didn't have them with us. Fortunately our hotel was close by and when we returned, buying tickets – at counter ten – became straightforward.

That had been two days before. Now, suddenly everyone at the station roused themselves and became animated. People surged through a tiny gate and onto the platform. We joined them and didn't have too much trouble identifying the only Upper Class compartment. The inside of the carriage was bile-green, smeared with the grime of decades. The four tiny ceiling fans for the whole compartment looked inadequate but weren't moving anyway. We examined our flimsy tickets which said we'd been allotted seats *ɔ* and *j*. There was evidence that the seats had once been reclinable and had built-in cushioning. This was disintegrating but at least it had been re-covered in stout military-green cloth. Some of the tray tables still almost functioned. This was really, really not Upper Class travel but it was going to be a small adventure.

Six o'clock on the dot, the train gave a lurch then, as if reluctant to start, almost imperceptibly began to move. A large bat, beautifully silhouetted against the rose of dawn, overtook the train. Through the open windows I saw once-white concrete tenements festooned with feisty little wall weeds, drying laundry and yet more razor wire. I caught snippets of unintelligible conversations. The speed increased from walking pace to perhaps thirty miles per hour, which caused the poor old train to creek and rattle and crash.

We were soon clear of Yangon city and looked out across the vast fertile delta of the Irrawaddy. I stuck my head out of the window for a better view, narrowly missing a mouthful of red spit emanating from a betel-chewing chap further up the train. The lush countryside was flat as flat, dotted with tiny thatched houses on stilts and the occasional breast-shaped pagoda. Women in big-brimmed hats squatted in paddy fields, planting. People moved about on ox-carts, bicycles, motorbikes, scooter-trucks, two-wheeled ploughs and other improvised modes of transport. We passed a line of ducks waddling purposely towards a drainage ditch. Giant pods dangled from big-buttressed kapok trees. Flame of the forest and red silk-cotton trees were in glorious bloom. Some bore white blossoms which took to the air, screaming, as they transformed into egrets. I heard a *whoop whoop whoop whoop whoop kok-kok kok-kok kok-kok kok-kok kok-kok-oo kok-kok-oo* – the familiar mad call of the coucal clearly audible above the rattle of the carriages.

A handsome man in a white shirt, with a bleached quiff and a big smile, was moving through our carriage speaking earnestly to each passenger in turn. He had the kind of obsequiousness I associate with evangelists. When he came to us, he handed us a small tract. I thought of refusing until I realised this was the breakfast menu. We could choose from:

Deep fried sparrow
Deep fried eel
Fried Rice
French toast
On Toast
Hard boil egg
Red Bull
Shark

Normally I'd have ordered something as unusual as sparrow but I love these cheeky little birds so chose On Toast instead. Further into our travels I worked out that nouns are sometimes lost in translation, so a café will advertise TEA – SNACK – COLD or COFFEE & COLD. Deep fried sparrow was actually sparrow bananas – the tasty little yellow ones. On Toast proved to be two fried eggs on white sliced bread. And Shark was simply an energy drink. We enjoyed our On Toast and managed to gulp down glasses of over-sweet Nescafé without spilling much despite the train lurching at random.

A three-year-old boy in front had been studying us with great seriousness over the back of his seat. I wondered if he was frightened of us but his face broke out into a sunshine smile when I shared some segments of orange with him. His mum turned to grin at us too when she saw where the fruit had come from. I wished we had a language in common. Everyone seemed genuinely friendly and always returned our attempts at a greeting, which sounded something like 'mingle about'. Folks were even more interested when they learned we were English. I took this as a colonial connection but of course that was not it. They smiled, and exclaimed 'Manchester United!', 'Wayne Rooney!' and 'Chelsea!'

The train stopped often but never for long. Food-sellers strode through the train with huge trays balanced on their heads, never dropping anything, shouting in Myanmar. The only one I understood was an old man who used three languages, 'Ye, *paani*, water, *ye.*' That '*paani*' was the only time I heard Hindi spoken.

Over some sections, the train rocked from side to side, but mostly it dodged and bucked like a wild creature trying to make a break for freedom. After one especially big jolt, water – fortunately clean – poured through the roof behind us. The supply to the loo was incontinent. This, of course, made me think I had to 'go'. I'd been putting this off as I wasn't confident my knees would allow me to pee without mishap.

My knees are worn out from too many Himalayan treks. I'd had surgery and stem cell treatment to my right knee six months earlier and my surgeon had forbidden what he called 'deep squats'. No problem, I thought: life in the UK seldom requires deep squats. I'd worked hard on my rehabilitation exercises (at least in the first two months) and re-strengthened my quadriceps and practised the balances my physio had suggested. I'd returned to cycling and hardly needed to wear my knee brace but could see that using the lavatory was going to demand some special skills.

It was clean but there was, of course, no pedestal (and certainly no loo paper) and there was also nothing to hang on to. I am a veteran of squat loos, so normally this wouldn't be a problem, but I'd rather neglected my exercises in the month before this trip. And a half squat was difficult to maintain while guarding against head injuries due to random train lurches. Looking at the speeding track down the modest hole between my legs induced a touch of vertigo too. I told myself to man up and cursed my idleness. Other silver travellers know the wisdom of pre-trip conditioning, and so should I.

Eventually I emerged with a bruised elbow but dry-knickered and unsullied. I even managed a well-directed and very refreshing bottom splosh with the scoop provided.

The smiley man with the bleached quiff came by often and when a passenger made a lip-smacking kissing noise, it took a moment to realise this was not a proposition but the accepted way to attract his attention. Smiley was kept busy bringing boxes of delicious-smelling, thoroughly fried, unrecognisable food. Sadly when we tried to order 'some of that' by pointing and smiling a lot, they cooked especially for us and it didn't seem as good.

The countryside changed. Low hills appeared on both horizons and, now that we had left the delta, the land was parched. This was a tough region for scratching out a living. We had a map but it wasn't easy to follow our progress northwards when we couldn't read most of the signage.

The temperature had now risen to around forty degrees Celsius and sweat dribbled from my nose and down my back. Someone started the ceiling fans but they were completely ineffectual. We had to drink water, but the train continued to buck like an unbroken horse and I wondered if trying to rise to the trot might make me spill less. All I achieved was to dislodge the blocks that served as my seat cushions.

There were often huge crashes as one compartment was wrenched out of synch with others. Some jolts left one carriage more than half a metre higher than its neighbour. It genuinely seemed only a matter of time before there would be a derailment. It amused us that 384 kyats of the 9,500 kyat ticket price was for life insurance. Even so, the whole ticket price was less than for one stop on the London Underground. Still, it was clear why so few people – locals or tourists – travelled this way.

At Pyinmana Junction a bevy of smartly dressed police and soldiers joined us. Alarmingly one carried a machine gun; two others held rifles that might have seen service during the Korean War. Their uniforms were crisp – as soon as these military men had decided on seats, they removed their shirts and dangled them with their weapons. I realised that we'd reached ten-year-old Naypyidaw, Royal City of the Sun, which is now the national capital. As we crossed several empty five-lane highways, we wondered why, if the planners really anticipated serious levels of traffic, these were interrupted by level crossings. Twelve hours into our ten-and-a-half-hour journey vendors offered chilled Myanmar and Tiger beers and half bottles of Grand Royal or High Class whiskies. We gazed out at a spectacular sunset, feeling ready for a sundowner. A can of Tiger hit the spot, and we rattled into Mandalay after fifteen hours, battered, sweaty and bruised of bum, mellow and ready to do battle for a taxi.

Dr Jane Wilson-Howarth's Nepal memoir *A Glimpse of Eternal Snows*, published in the UK by Bradt, is 'the proverbial life-changing book' (*Daily Telegraph*). Jane co-wrote *Your Child Abroad: a Travel Health Guide* and contributed to the health chapters of many Bradt guides.  Now of pensionable age, she continues to work as a GP in Cambridge and lectures widely: www.wilson-howarth.com

Final Journey in Sierra Leone
Ed Bridge

Nothing had gone smoothly whilst I was backpacking around upcountry Sierra Leone. One of the journeys had taken over twelve hours when I was expecting six or seven; it included a spine-jarring, muscle-aching ride crammed into a minibus. I concluded that, at sixty-six, I was too old for this sort of travel. And this time I couldn't be late: I had to catch my plane home. I was also on edge for another reason. You see, my home team Manchester United was playing its closest rivals Chelsea in a vital end-of-season match that afternoon.

I was in Makeni, over a hundred miles away from Lungi Airport. It was the end of a month of reawakening happy memories of the country where I lived forty-eight years ago, when I taught with Voluntary Service Overseas at a college. I had enquired about staying at a motel which was run by Ernest Kamara. It turned out he had started his teacher training at the same college in 1964, a few months after I had left. Even so, he insisted on telling people that I was 'his teacher' and kindly arranged for me to visit my old college and familiar sights in nearby Magburaka, driven by his friend George, a college alumnus. Ernest also said he would make sure I got to the airport in time.

The standard route to the airport was to take the road to Freetown, a rust-bucket ferry across the river to Tagrin and then a

104

taxi. My recent experience, however, suggested that multiple modes of transport increased the risk of delays. So I opted for the road route via Port Loko. My trusty Bradt guidebook assured me it was possible, even though it might be a bit slower and less comfortable.

I turned up at Ernest's motel compound shortly after midday. He was not there but, as the flight was a late night one, I was not particularly worried. When he did arrive, in the course of the next hour or so he came up with three or four proposals which all involved the ferry. I emphasised that I wanted to go all the way by road and he went away to reconsider.

When he came back, he tried to dissuade me by telling me my idea would cost a hundred dollars. Considering I had not paid very much for my hotels, I decided that I could afford it and accepted the proposition. Ernest started phoning around and the next thing I knew, a money changer had arrived. He converted my American dollars into a large wad of leones.

Soon after, two men arrived at the compound and told me that they had a car for my airport journey outside. It looked all right to me and, happy as Larry, I handed over the wad. I was overjoyed that, with hours to spare, things were moving smoothly at last. Then they told me it would take some time to find a driver.

It took about half an hour for a driver to appear and it was explained that the car could only take me after a complete oil change. So I got in and the driver took us into the busy streets of Makeni. A garage with an inspection pit was found, we waited our turn to use it, and the car was driven onto the ramp above the pit. For the next twenty minutes or so I remained in my seat seemingly in mid-air whilst things happened below me. I was beginning to feel more than a little uneasy.

When we set off again, we headed for a petrol station on the edge of town and joined the inevitable queue of cars and motorbikes. Time just went by as it often does in Sierra Leone. Eventually, we started off down the road. I presumed that we were now on our way. Wrong again! After a couple of minutes we pulled onto the side of the road. The driver just said we were waiting for someone.

Although we were probably there for only ten minutes, it seemed an awful lot longer. Then who should appear but George. He clambered in and sat on the back seat without explanation. I could only presume that Ernest had arranged for me to be accompanied to ensure that I would reach the airport safely. Anyway, about two hours after my car had arrived, with most of my contingency time now gone, we were on the move and finally left the environs of Makeni.

The first part of the route was on a tarmac highway so we moved at a fair rate. While not entirely relaxed, I began to feel more confident that we would make it in time. I chatted to George about the football. If United won, I explained, they would likely gain another league title, giving them a record nineteen titles. That meant they would overtake the one set by arch-rivals Liverpool.

All good things must come to an end, and after a while we had to turn off the highway. Suddenly, things were a lot different. For a start there was no longer a road as such. A new road was being built and for half an hour we slid about on earthworks that were going to provide the base of it. We kept going at a reduced rate but at least without any traffic problems as ours was the only car.

Then we turned onto the road to Port Loko. We were now at times down to a snail's pace in order to avoid potholes. There was little I could do but to grin and bear it.

We came to the quiet town of Port Loko and stopped outside an establishment run by a relative of the driver. Amongst other things it sold beer. I bought a bottle each for the three of us so that the driver could take a well-earned break. Trying not to think of the passing time, I asked if anyone knew the latest score from Old Trafford. A man volunteered that he had heard United were 1-0 up, but this was quite a bit earlier. Would they stay ahead?

Progress out of Port Loko continued to be slow going. When we approached habitation and I was spotted in the car, the cry of 'Porto' went up from children outside. Just as I found in other remote parts, the kids would line the road, chant 'Porto, Porto' and wave madly. Some would try and run alongside the car. I would respond with equally frantic waving. It is believed that Pedro da Cintra, a Portuguese explorer, gave Sierra Leone its name in the fifteenth century whilst sailing down the Atlantic coast, and white men are referred to as Portos despite no Portuguese presence on the land, as far as I know.

At 7.30 p.m. it became dark and I gained the impression that we were travelling even more slowly. My anxiety level was mounting as I was supposed to check in by 9 p.m. Eventually, however, we reached the streets and lights of Lungi. For the first time in ages we saw other traffic, most of it heading for the airport. We joined them and nudged our way towards the car park. I relaxed. We were arriving in time for the plane with just under an hour to spare.

As we approached the terminal, George directed the driver to stop close to a waiting girl. We got out and George introduced me to his daughter. Clearly she had recently flown in and it became obvious that George had really come along to give her a free lift back home.

For some reason, I couldn't resist asking her if she knew the football result. Surprisingly, she did. United had beaten Chelsea 2–1.

It then hit me how wonderful life was. I had had a great holiday with a few adventures, despite the fraught journeys. I had been thrilled that morning to visit the classroom where I had taught nearly fifty years ago. I was relieved to be in time for the plane home and the icing on the cake was that United were almost certainly going to be Premiership champions.

I thanked her for the good news and, with high emotion, I asked if I could give her a kiss.

'No way,' she replied. 'I support Liverpool!'

Ed Bridge was born in Manchester in 1945. After school he spent a year teaching with VSO in Sierra Leone. He returned home to take a Maths degree, followed by a thirty-five year career in computing. Now a grandfather, he is retired, living near Bristol and volunteering for Citizens Advice.

Does he still think he is too old to ever get into a packed minibus to travel over rough roads again? Of course not. Aches and pains are transient; memories are forever.

Danger in Diyarbakir
Eithne Nightingale

At the sound of gunfire I wake from an anxious dream and get out of bed. Perhaps I should have followed the advice to turn down this invitation to Diyarbakir in southeast Turkey. The heavy police presence has already made me nervous. But I could not resist the opportunity to visit the longest-surviving walled city in the world.

I edge towards the window and peer through the curtains into the dark. I need not have worried. These are not incursions over the border from Assad's Syrian regime or terrorist activities of the PKK. They are fireworks to celebrate a local Kurdish wedding. Rockets zoom over the towers and turrets of the city walls. Spinning balls of fire light up the minarets and cascades of multi-coloured sparklers crackle into nothingness.

I rise early to meet Zerda, a young Kurdish woman, who insists on taking me for a traditional Diyarbakir breakfast. We climb the steps to the top storey of the city's busiest inn, Hasan Pasa Hani. This striped basalt and white alabaster building, typical of the architecture of the city, was a major stopping place on both the Silk Road and the Spice Route. The manager, bristling a fine walrus moustache, shows us to our seats overlooking the central fountain.

'A left-wing activist,' says Zerda. 'You can tell by his moustache.' Leaning over the balcony she points out the significance of the different styles: the drooping right-wing moustache of the jeweller, the curling moustache of the Alevi carpet seller and the long moustaches of the Kurds.

My education in facial hair is interrupted by the arrival of waitresses in coloured headscarves, bearing four or five dishes at a time. Pungent Kurdish cheese braided into plaits; mammoth roasted red peppers and plump aubergines; wheat fried with butter, a local delicacy; assorted eggs and chunks of lamb; sheep's yoghurt and a dazzling array of honey, molasses and jams – pomegranate and pear, apple and apricot, mulberry and watermelon. All twenty-eight dishes are mopped up with huge ovals of homemade bread and washed down with mint tea followed by wild pistachio coffee.

'And now for a walk through the bazaar and along the ramparts,' says Zerda.

'But I can hardly move,' I protest.

But Zerda is insistent.

'Leave your valuables in your room,' she warns. 'Tourists are likely to be robbed or attacked.'

After stopping off at my hotel, facing a huge mural of Ataturk, we walk through the bazaar. Tradesmen trundle cartloads of mammoth watermelons down cobbled alleyways, knocking over buckets of yoghurt. Stiff mannequins, draped in traditional bridal dress, stare out at us from glittering textile emporiums. Old men beat hammers against copper kettles, carve Koran holders out of wood and mould donkey saddles out of leather. Young boys try, but fail, to sell us Che Guevara T-shirts and football scarves of the local team. In the cheese market I recoil at overpowering odours but admire the twisted coils of goat's cheese. In the spice market I sniff the red, orange and ochre pyramids, identifying each, and taste the mounds of sticky chilli paste. Zerda leads me through the Armenian quarter, the Christian quarter, the Kurdish and Arab quarters, dropping snippets of this city's rich history as we go. Finally we reach the splendid Urfa Gate.

The walls are five kilometres of magnificence, two storeys high, punctuated with eighty-two towers of which all but five are intact. But my balance is not as good as it used to be. My knees are not as strong. As we climb up the crumbling steps to the top, stones slip from under my feet.

'Are you sure it's safe?' I ask, grabbing Zerda's arm.

'Of course,' she laughs. 'I've been coming up here since I was a child. Mind you,' she adds, 'the walls do need some repair. Some of the refugees have taken stones to build their homes.'

She points to makeshift shacks outside the city walls. Many of the refugees have migrated from the surrounding countryside to escape the war between the PKK and the Turkish government. I hold onto Zerda even tighter. I say nothing of my weak knees, my increasing fear of heights or my horror at the destruction of the city's heritage dating back to the Romans.

As the path widens I gain more confidence and let go of Zerda. I gaze over narrow alleys and the cloistered courtyards of the old city. I listen to the muezzin from the minarets. I breathe in the fragrance rising from the lemon trees below. The view outside the city walls is a different matter. Lines of washing hang over flat-roofed houses built out of rubble. A forest of satellite dishes litters the sky.

'People round here don't watch the official Turkish channel, even though there is now a Kurdish language version,' says Zerda. It used to be against the law to speak Kurdish or even sing Kurdish songs.

'Why don't they watch the Kurdish version?' I ask

'They don't trust the government.'

After a good hour I take Zerda's arm again and we climb slowly down the steps into another part of the city. At the bottom an old man, fingering his *subha* beads, grasps Zerda's hand, repeating the same words over and over again. When he finally lets go I ask what he said.

'May Allah bless the Kurds. They have suffered too much.' She explains that the old man lost most of his family when his village was bombed in the 1990s and that his only son is still missing. 'Everyone here has lost someone close to them.'

My own anxieties about being caught up in a terrorist attack, of being robbed or of slipping from the city walls, fade in comparison.

'My friend Ilhami will take you to the airport tomorrow,' says Zerda. 'Be ready at ten o'clock.'

But it is Zerda, not Ilhami, who comes to pick me up the following morning.

'Ilhami had to go to the hospital,' she says, avoiding my gaze. 'His niece fell off the walls. Just where we were yesterday, near Urfa Gate.'

Eithne Nightingale is a writer, photographer, storyteller and researcher. She writes travel articles, memoir and fiction and is currently researching child migration to East London. She previously worked at the Victoria and Albert Museum and co-edited *Museums, Equality and Social Justice* (Routledge 2012). She has been successful in several literary competitions. See eithnenightingale.wordpress.com.

No Risk, No Fun

Roger Bray

The German language is notorious for multi-syllable nouns. The only redeeming feature on the day I broke my *Oberschenkelknochenhals* was a moment of unintended flattery. The surgeon who was to operate on my hip mistakenly took me for sixty. Six months earlier, in the company of several other aging skiers, I had marked my seventieth.

Disaster struck at about 11 a.m. on 18th January 2013. It was a gorgeous morning in the Austrian Arlberg resort of Lech, the sort of morning that reminds you that life is too brief to fritter away. Thus breakfast was a tug of priorities between our desire to linger a little longer over the Hotel Gotthard's splendid buffet and impatience to get out on the new snow under a sky of cloudless cobalt.

There was the usual struggle to get my boots on. In a mad rush of self-indulgence I'd had them custom fitted, at vast expense, at a shop in the Rocky Mountains. My excuse? I have difficult feet, liable to blister. OK, said my wife, but they'll have to see you out. The first time I wore them was a revelation. I felt I had only to raise an eyebrow to make a perfectly carved turn.

Those boots certainly weren't made for walking but mercifully it was only a short clump down the main street to the Rüfikopf cable car station, where we elbowed our way into a packed cabin, disgorging with a sense of joyous release at 2,362 metres and setting off down the wide piste that is the first descent on the Weisse – or White – Ring.

This circuit, mostly linked by lifts, would take us first to Zürs and then back to Lech on the opposite side of the valley. That was the plan at least.

The previous day the cloud had been so thick, and visibility so limited, that I had skied off the edge of that same run, plunging headfirst into fresh powder and struggling up again, giggling like an old fool. Today you could see for miles. This was surely not a morning for such daft mishaps.

As a skier with over forty-five years' experience I didn't feel particularly accident-prone, though there had been a few nasty spills. In my late fifties I had lost my memory in Colorado, after a fall that threw my head back with a whiplash effect. I skied without knowing it for an hour or so but returned to the world of the sentient as I was carted to the clinic on a stretcher. The doctor called it retrograde amnesia, common in car crashes, charged me $200 and discharged me. In my early sixties I broke my wrist in Andorra after hitting something under the snow. The worst effect of a forearm in plaster was that I couldn't uncork a bottle of wine for six weeks.

These days I enjoyed feeling completely in control. Falls were rarer. As a friend put it, I had reached the ripe age at which, when you tell passing acquaintances you still ski, their patronizing reply is, 'Good for you.'

We branched off the circuit to take a tempting run of intermediate difficulty. It was steep enough to make the knees work and we had it all to ourselves. My skis were doing exactly as they were told.

But a little further down, towards Zürs, we had a minor marital disagreement about which piste to take and ended up on the route of the annual Weisse Ring race, which was to take place next day.

It was hardly a challenging run, but competitors were out practising and it was congested. After about a hundred metres it made a sharp dogleg to the left. I decided to make that turn on the wide outside of the bend. I wasn't in any hurry after all. The next thing I remember is seeing my left ski wavering as if with a mind of its own – and I was dumped ferociously on the snow.

I suspect someone travelling faster than me may have clipped the back of my ski. I attempted to stand up but immediately collapsed. I felt acute pain followed by a sense of bewilderment. Everything seemed to happen in slow motion. A passing ski instructor interrupted his private lesson to call for emergency assistance. He comforted me while we waited. An akia, the sledge-cum-stretcher used to ferry injured skiers off the mountain, soon arrived.

Did they give me morphine at the clinic in Lech? I can't remember. My boots were eased off painlessly, as though they were several sizes too big. I was still hoping against hope that I might have just jarred my leg badly. But then the doctor in charge returned with an X-ray. The narrow neck of bone below my left hip joint was broken. Mightn't it mend of its own accord? I asked wishfully. No. I would need to undergo an operation, spend a week in hospital and then keep my weight off it for three months. All sorts of miseries and complications swam before my eyes.

When you suffer a ski injury an invisible meter starts running. It's like throwing a wad of twenty-pound notes to a ravening horde. I was already more than four hundred pounds poorer before they had even lifted me onto the operating table. At this point I was past caring – but don't let anyone talk you into going uninsured.

The hospital consultant told me he might have to fit an artificial hip. Could today get any better? I wondered aloud. He looked again at the X-rays. My bone density was good. Maybe he could screw the bone together instead. Did he have my permission to fit the new hip if that proved impracticable? He went next door to confer with a colleague. 'Well,' I heard him say as the anaesthetic began to take effect, 'no risk, no fun.'

Next morning the horizon began to brighten slightly. 'Bit of luck,' he said as he looked in on his round. 'Good as new.' He had pinned the bone with three whopping titanium bolts. The blood supply to the hip joint might dry up at any time over the next couple of years but the longer it didn't the less it was likely to. Could I ski again? No reason why not. What about running, which was most likely the foundation of my healthy bone density? That would be safe as long as I used well-cushioned shoes.

My e-reader relieved the boredom of staring at the ceiling and thinking of all the ways the fall could have been avoided. Friends sent sympathetic texts. I attempted to communicate with my ward mate, an Austrian with a cough like a stuttering two-stroke, but efforts to resolve my High German with his opaque dialect made me feel like a BBC news reader in the Gorbals.

Travelling home was a doddle but hopping upstairs, especially last thing after a drink or two, was a nightmare. I couldn't get out to meetings. People just had to come to me. It might sound good, sitting on your backside, being waited on, reading, listening to music, watching the telly – until you have to do it. Even a tricky outing to a shopping centre coffee shop relieved the tedium.

After about seven weeks of this I went for a check-up at a south London hospital. You can walk on it, they said. Now I didn't want to look a gift horse in the mouth but hadn't the Austrians said three months? 'We take a different view,' said the consultant. 'By the way,' he asked, looking at the notes, 'do you break something every time you go skiing?'

Walking on it proved a tentative process. My physiotherapist counselled patience. By late May, while I was still exercising to rebuild strength in my wasted leg, we flew to Mallorca. There's nothing like a spell of confinement to make you appreciate the pleasures of travel. We wandered in Palma, and I even managed to hike, apprehensively, on a steep, rubble-strewn trail in the countryside. In mid-summer we returned by car to the scene of the crime, walked on the now snowless slopes, and collected our equipment. Joy at being able to hike again in the mountains was unconfined.

By December I felt ready to try skiing once more but I was nervous. If it happened again, I thought, I really would be plunged into sedentary old age. But it was another of those glorious, crystal clear days in the Alps that reminds you of life's brevity, so I bit the bullet.

Within hours I was skiing with a certain insouciance again. In some respects, I mused, the mind is like a blackboard, wiped clean after each lesson. Well, almost clean. Down at the bottom of mine the German word for my upper femur survives, indelibly chalked: *Der Oberschenkelknochenhals.*

Roger Bray has been writing about travel for over forty years. A former travel editor of London's *Evening Standard* and frequent broadcaster, he is the joint author of *Flight to the Sun*, a definitive history of the post-war tourism boom, and has won a number of awards for his writing.

The Bad Luck Pagoda
Keith Baillie

Travelling is not all roses. I was visiting Bagan in Myanmar. My last visit was thirty-some years before, when I was in my early thirties and they were called Pagan and Burma. This morning I wanted to visit a number of the two thousand or so temples scattered throughout the surrounding plains.

When travelling, I often hire a motorcycle taxi – with a driver, because I do not know how to ride a motorbike. However, Bagan bans motorcycle taxis – perhaps due to liability considerations – leaving tourists the option of self-driven electric bicycles known as 'e-bikes', expensive automobile taxis, or expensive, slow and bumpy horse-drawn carriages. So of course I rented an e-bike. Lacking gears, it looked simple enough, and I started well, navigating my way to various temples by road and sandy trail.

I had my first fall about an hour into the day. Neither I nor the e-bike was badly injured, so I told myself that it was the inevitable learning experience.

A few temples later I had my second fall. This one ripped my trouser leg and scraped my knee raw – rather painful when climbing hundreds of temple steps. It also bent one of the pedals so it would not turn, although fortunately pedals are only needed if the battery runs out. I tied my handkerchief around the wound and had a beer to steady my nerves before continuing.

All this transpired before I had even visited the Dhammayangyi Pahto, known locally as the Bad Luck Pagoda! This is the largest temple on the Bagan plain, resembling an Egyptian step pyramid. It was built in the twelfth century by the cruel King Narathu, who ascended the throne by murdering his father and brother. According to legend, masons were executed if a needle could be pushed between the bricks. Eventually he was himself assassinated in the temple and the workers filled the interior with brick rubble to block access to the terraces. Fortunately, my visit was uneventful and I lived to tell the tale.

However, continuing my circuit, potholes and sandy patches attracted my e-bike like magnetic fields, despite my efforts to avoid them. Chains of potholes set the e-bike in resonance so it jumped around like a bucking bronco. Hence it wasn't long before I had my third fall. This grazed my other leg and bent the other pedal. At this, I decided I should admit defeat and never rent an e-bike again. But I still had to get the damned thing back to the rental shop.

As darkness fell, I found myself on a dual carriageway with cars and trucks honking as they sped by. Alas, e-bikes have no rearview mirrors. I also had to avoid e-bikes parked without lights on the side of the highway, and coming into town had to steer around pedestrians and motorbikes approaching on *my side* of the road. Fortunately I found a mechanic to hammer out the bent pedals, before returning the e-bike in one piece. The rental shop owner asked if I'd like to rent the e-bike the next day. I replied, somewhat dishonestly, that I'd think about it.

I returned to my hotel, looking forward to a shower and a chance to recover from the stresses of the day. As requested, the hotel staff had moved my bags to a quieter room. Entering the room, I noticed a soft, thin conical object on the floor and threw it in the bin. Later I found the rest of the gecko, tailless and immobile – at first I thought from shock, but my scare tactics elicited no response, and I concluded it was dead. I can tolerate sharing my room with another live being, but not with a dead one. I asked the hotel staff to remove the dead gecko and, while about it, fix the air conditioning and toilet flush and provide toilet paper (I'm picky, I know). Later I noticed a large number of small flying insects in my room, presumably because the room gecko was not performing its customary duties, so I requested a replacement gecko – a live one this time. The hotel staff seemed baffled; maybe the language barrier.

I spent the rest of my evening tending my wounds, sewing my trouser leg back together and arranging a horse carriage for the next day's sunrise – and writing this, so I remember never to rent an e-bike again.

A native Brit, **Keith Baillie** had a career in technical writing and education that spanned four continents, while his wanderlust has taken him to over sixty countries. Now retired in San Francisco, he continues to travel extensively, especially in southeast Asia, taking photographs and sometimes doing volunteer work.

Daring to Do Something Different

Thumbs Up
Hilary Bradt

A few days ago I was standing in a lay-by, feeling a little foolish – as one does – with my thumb out, watching drivers lean forward in their seats to stare intently before deciding no, and speeding on.

No-one does it these days, they tell me, but I'm proud to say that I've hitchhiked every decade of my life except the first. And I'm in my seventies. I hitch when there is no alternative, as was the case last week, but I also hitch because it's the best way I know to meet thoroughly decent people and reaffirm my trust in the human race. I also think it's interesting to experience the shifting ground between control and helplessness.

For my generation, hitchhiking was part of life. We all did it. As youngsters, few of us had cars and public transport was expensive. If we wanted to travel abroad we hitchhiked and competed over who could spend the least amount of money on their holiday. When a friend and I travelled to the Middle East in 1963, we were honour-bound never to pay for transport. Nor did we need to.

Then I moved to America and assumed that my hitchhiking days were over. All Americans have cars, don't they? So I was in for a shock when I starting dating a man who not only had no car, but assumed that I would hitch everywhere with him. I didn't like to say no, so there I was, in my thirties, exploring America through the kindness of strangers. And such extravagant kindness! One driver just pointed out his house, got out of the car and said, 'You kids go see this place. Just bring the car back later this evening.' Yes, we were kids to him.

As I continued to seek the occasional lift in my forties and fifties, the drivers must have got a nasty shock when they stopped and realised that this hitchhiker was getting on in years. But it was only when I started travelling with Janice, who is two years older than me and has white hair, that I discovered the advantages of flaunting, rather than concealing, your age.

She also had hitchhiked as a youngster, in Greece, so when we planned a return visit to the Mani Peninsula to see some of her favourite places, we agreed that the once-a-day bus wasn't going to get us far and we would hitchhike when necessary. I hadn't realised how easy it would be. I'd push Janice to the front, and cars would stop because what else can you do when a white-haired old lady sticks her thumb out and looks beseeching – and is carrying a sign to the destination written in the Greek alphabet as well as in English? They stopped. They all stopped. We rode with a priest, with his hat and his little bun, and Janice chatted to him in Greek (don't ask, she just seems to know all the European languages and a smattering of African ones); we travelled with some German tourists and exchanged information on the most rewarding Byzantine churches, with a talkative woman lawyer, and finally hopped onto the back of a pick-up truck to join two young Albanians who, we gathered, were employed on a building site.

The Albanians spoke about the same level of Greek as Janice, so although conversation didn't exactly flow, it sputtered along quite happily. They were, understandably, very curious about why two women who certainly looked past the first flush of youth were hitchhiking. They muttered among themselves, casting furtive glances at us before asking Janice her age; sixty-two she told them. No interest there then. So they pointed to me. 'How old is she?' You could imagine a little glimmer of hope that I was a very wrinkly thirty-eight-year-old. Once the truth was out they took no further interest in us. We relaxed, until another pick-up approached from the opposite direction, and to our alarm a hand with a gun appeared though its window.

Oh, it was a joke, was it? Of course it was. The rest of the journey was uneventful.

Another time we had a wonderful ride in a bread van, enveloped in the smell of freshly-baked loaves, and exchanging *kalimeras* with astonished-looking customers. It was clear that hitchhiking in one's sixties is not just as good, but better than all those decades ago when we all did it.

On subsequent travels in England, we walked long stretches of the South West Coast Path and hitched back to our B&B. For me it was as good as being in Greece again, sitting in the back and letting Janice chat away in French to the Parisians who had stopped for us. They had assumed, as so often happens, that we were in some sort of trouble. Once they recovered from their astonishment, they learned all about Cornwall and we got to Penzance after the last bus had gone. Perfect! It made the journey into more of an adventure and we saw our country from another perspective.

So when we celebrated the introduction of concessionary bus passes by travelling the breadth of England free of charge, we planned sometimes to substitute bus travel for thumb travel.

The first time was on a rural road. One thing I've learned through all these decades of hitching is that the quieter the road, the better the chance of getting a lift. Sure enough, on a country lane in Norfolk the first car stopped and a concerned-looking man asked if we were OK. Once he'd come to terms with the fact that we were hitchhikers he went out of his way, literally, to be helpful, taking us the scenic route to our destination, past a stately home so we could peer down the driveway. The next time, however, was not so easy.

We'd actually booked a place to stay at our final destination, Lowestoft – up until then it had been pot luck – and all the buses had stopped running at teatime. As they do: the time available for bus-pass travel is quite restricted. We had come prepared with some cardboard and a felt-tipped pen so we could sign our destination, and we added 'please' to show what nice polite ladies we were.

As we stood there waiting, and waiting, I thought how I'd never had a really bad experience hitchhiking. Boring, yes, alarming, maybe, but never terrifying. My confidence in strangers has been liberating, life-enhancing. Maybe I have been lucky, but I wonder if it is actually any more dangerous these days than when I first nervously put out my thumb to a passing car at the age of eighteen. We just think it is, and that limits our freedom.

The road to Lowestoft was a main road, however, and, as happens on main roads, everyone sped past. This was not really much fun. We stood there for forty-five minutes, smiling inanely and feeling silly. Then a van stopped. We grabbed our rucksacks, ran up to the passenger window, and asked where he was going. That's what I've always done, and the emotion never changes. Resignation or gloom transforms into hope and gratitude, as it did outside Axminster last week, when I needed to retrieve my car after a walk. A young man stopped, welcomed me in, and my trust in people's goodness was yet again reaffirmed.

Since writing the first Bradt guide in 1974, **Hilary Bradt** has made travel her business, working as a writer, lecturer and tour leader. In this latter capacity she has encountered intrepid oldies who convinced her that age is no barrier to adventure. In 2008 she was awarded an MBE and  the following year a Lifetime Achievement Award from the British Guild of Travel Writers. She is currently working on the final volume of a trilogy of *Slow Travel* guides to Devon – hence the need occasionally to hitch a lift.

Plodding to the Far Northwest

Rosemary Fretwell

'People have *died* out here,' he said darkly. This statement only increased our determination to carry on. He tried again: 'Supposing it snows.' At this I nearly laughed, for it was not at all cold despite the wind. And it was the end of June.

'Hadn't you better give this up? You still have a long way to go. You haven't reached the lighthouse yet, and then you'll have to turn into the teeth of the wind.' But it had stopped raining an hour ago, the wind had lessened, the sky was brighter and the forecast was for it to improve throughout the afternoon and evening.

This was the fourth attempt by the minibus driver to make us give in and pay him to transport us back to civilisation. We didn't want to go back to civilisation, we wanted to go on to civilisation – our car, parked four miles beyond Sandwood Bay with flasks of tea and chocolate biscuits in the boot. We would have liked to believe that he was really concerned for our safety, that he considered us a couple of old codgers who thought they were going for a gentle stroll, and didn't want to get involved in the rescue when we inevitably came to grief. But we couldn't forget the look of annoyance on his face earlier that morning on the ferry when he was collecting fares for his minibus and we announced that we didn't need his services because we intended to walk to Cape Wrath lighthouse, then out via Sandwood Bay.

We were already two-thirds of the way to the lighthouse on the track which snaked away across the hills ahead. It was bleak. Wild. Windy. In the distance we could see a glowing sandy beach with teetering rock stacks peeping out behind a knoll. We were completely on our own – except when the minibuses passed us every half hour.

Colin and I may have been in our dotage (well, sixties actually) but we had planned this hike in minute detail. It was part of our retirement project, to walk the entire coast of mainland Britain. We had started in Bognor Regis eleven years before when we turned left at the pier and continued walking. We may have had many breaks in time during which we had returned to the comforts of home, but we hadn't had any breaks in the route. So far we had walked every inch of the way and we weren't going to give up now because a minibus driver was vexed.

'Do you think you ought to continue?' he persisted. 'You're very slow, you've been walking four hours and you've only done eight miles.' So? That is our pace – two miles an hour including stops. Everything is going to plan.

'This is the last minibus back to the ferry which will be the final one across the estuary today. You'd better hop in, this is your last chance to get back.' For the fourth time, we assured our apparently concerned friend that we were aware of the challenges we faced, that we had maps and compasses and knew how to use them, that we knew where the bothies were and would shelter in them if the weather turned nasty, that we had extra food and water in our rucksacks, and that we had informed two quite separate people of what we were doing so that if we didn't turn up tomorrow they would send out search parties.

He shrugged his shoulders, saying, 'Well, at least you'll be able to buy hot drinks at the lighthouse.' Would we? How come? 'Because he's opened a café there.' Well, that was good news, we weren't expecting that.

It was a few more miles to the lighthouse, the halfway point, and it didn't seem to take us long. But that was the easy part – the second half would be much more challenging. An open doorway announced 'The Ozone', the new café. It had recently been opened by Princess Anne, we later learned, who had arrived and left by helicopter – no tramping across the moors for her, not even a ferry ride and a minibus. The owner of the café was friendly and encouraging when we explained what we were planning to do. He made us wonderful mugs of tea, then he insisted we get out our maps so he could show us the best way to proceed across the rough terrain ahead.

'Go back down the road for about a mile until you come to this bend. Veer out to avoid two gullies, then make for the col between those two hills. After that stay as close to the coast as the cliffs will allow – it is less boggy than inland and the grass is shorter.'

I asked him about the river we had to cross, marked with a double line on the map meaning it was more than a mere stream. He told us there were stepping stones. 'You'll see where other people have crossed,' he assured us. 'You'll be fine.' I was relieved, because the minibus driver had unnerved me. Meanwhile, a minibus with a different driver arrived with another bunch of tourists. So much for the last bus. We set off at three-thirty, and were passed by what was the last minibus of the day. Then we turned off the road, and felt very alone as we set off across the moors.

The ground was uneven and boggy, so we had to watch carefully where we were putting our feet as we used map and compass to take us south. We veered round the gullies, as instructed, but there were still a lot of downs and ups, and when we were down we had to rely on the compass to keep us straight. There were numerous streams to cross, finding the narrowest point to jump over or using rocks as stepping stones. Everywhere there were flowers, many of them typical bog plants, but the wild orchids were so prolific it was difficult not to trample them and they quite took our breath away – each tiny flower was exquisite.

After the gullies we climbed towards the col between two hills, and the spectacular coast began to reveal itself. We felt very privileged as few people see these views. Blue sky began to appear. It was still windy, but we had expected nothing else on this wild moor.

It seemed to take a long time to get up to the col. Every time we topped a ridge and thought that was it, another higher ridge appeared ahead. Although older than me, Colin is fitter and was always in front. I kept plodding along, remembering the advice of Sir Ranulph Fiennes who recently climbed Everest at the age of sixty-five. He said that he copes with long and difficult walks by plodding with no expectations. 'I don't think of the destination at all, I just keep plodding.' It kept me going even when I was weary.

We topped the col in the end, and down in the next valley we could see the fence of the MOD firing range. The way down was extremely steep and I had to zigzag. We crossed a rocky stream, then it was almost hands and knees to get up the other side. We climbed over a stile, and now the MOD range was behind us. We were halfway between the lighthouse and Sandwood Bay, and it had taken us three hours.

We were right by the coast now, walking along the top of the cliffs. The surf pounding below was invigorating, yet still we seemed to have a lot of climbing to do. Occasionally there was the vestige of a footpath but we couldn't make out whether it had been worn by humans or deer.

And the views – they were unbelievable. The minibus crowd miss all this. We felt fortunate to be fit enough to do this. When we finally got to the top of the last ridge, we had a wonderful panoramic view of Sandwood Bay ahead, not a building or a road in sight.

We began to descend, down and down until we reached the Strath Chailleach River. I had been right to be concerned. It was broader than any other stream we had crossed and it carried a lot of water. We couldn't find the stepping stones. There were lots of stones, but always a gap which was too wide for me to get across. Perhaps if I had been young and athletic I could have leapt over in a dozen or more places, but I'm old, lack binocular vision and have a back problem. Colin probably could have jumped across, but he knew my limitations, so he didn't.

We were both very tired by then. We knew there was a footbridge about two miles upstream but we didn't want to walk that far inland, especially as the ground became boggy as soon as we moved away from the coast. We must have spent half an hour assessing possible crossing points before Colin found one about half a mile upstream. The boulders were bigger there, and Colin was able to walk over. I didn't trust my balance, so I shuffled across on my backside.

We were over. I felt an enormous sense of relief – we were almost there. But not quite. The way to the coast was across boggy ground and we were half a mile inland. It took a long time; with every step we didn't know how deep our feet would sink. But the water never came over the tops of our boots and our feet remained dry. Eventually we stepped down onto a sandy beach. I felt a lot better by the pounding surf. Colin had noticed that the tide was going out and hoped it would ebb sufficiently for us to get round some protruding rocks into Sandwood Bay. His hunch paid off – there was just one pool, which he jumped and I ran through quickly so that the water didn't have time to get into my boots.

What a beautiful place was Sandwood Bay. If ever a spot on this earth could be described as heaven, this was it. We crossed a shallow river and then walked along the golden sands. We were the only people in a world untouched by man, a world shaped by the sea. It was already 10 p.m. and the sun was low over the water, giving everything a surreal orange glow. With the tide going out, the sand was pristine. We left footprints as we walked along, like treading in new snow. Yes, we were definitely in paradise.

We still had four-and-a-half miles to go, but we knew there was a proper path from there on. Reluctantly we left this idyllic place and made our way through the dunes as the sun sank slowly towards the horizon. We reached a grassy col where sheep grazed and the sun set at last. It gradually got dark, but never too gloomy to see where we were going. The path was well marked. We were both weary by now, but we kept 'plodding along' at an even pace. We crossed the moor and passed several lochans which we could just about see in the shadow.

It was less than a mile from the end of the walk when I tripped over a boulder and fell headlong into soft greenery. Fatigue had made me clumsy. I wasn't hurt, but Colin panicked – I think he had been on edge all day that I would fall and break my leg, or worse. I quickly reassured him, but I was winded and needed a few moments before I could get up.

Then we saw lights from houses… where people were living. We were fast approaching civilisation. I can't tell you how welcome that sight was. At the gate leading out to the road, we met a group of young people with large packs on their backs. They were the first people we had encountered since we left the lighthouse, nearly nine hours before.

A retired teacher, mother of four and grandmother of five, **Rosemary Fretwell** has been married to her husband, Colin, for forty-nine years. They both hate crowds and cities, but love wild places and are keen on photography and wildlife. Since 1998 they have been walking the  coastline of mainland Britain, and are currently about four-fifths of the way round.

A Horse Trek in Bhutan

Sue Bathurst

Time is not exactly running out but with sixty-nine years down, my horizons for trekking on horses will not extend. I was off on the first ever horse trek in Bhutan, between India and Tibet in the eastern Himalayas.

The number of pilots permitted to land at Paro, one of the most challenging airports in the world, can be counted on fingers. As the plane wove along valleys below the five thousand-metre peaks, with alternate wings dipped at forty-five degrees and farm workers looking down on us from their narrow terraces, it occurred to me there could be fewer more romantic places to meet one's end. However having watched the Queen Mother's shopping being weighed in at Kolkata, I rallied my confidence.

Bhutan is just over half the size of Scotland, with a population of 750,000, and the success of its government is famously not measured in GNP but in GNH – Gross National Happiness, last officially measured in 2010 by a forty-three page questionnaire completed by a representative ten per cent of the population. This guiding principle, combined with an almost entirely Buddhist population, makes for a relaxed atmosphere. We walked from the plane across the tarmac, stopping to take photographs of each other against the backdrop of the mountain corridor. National Security was not perceived to have been threatened; nobody objected; no-one's cameras were impounded. The airport buildings had the outward appearance of a country house hotel, with beautifully painted external timbers framing whitewashed panels. The laidback welcome continued as we passed through the official barriers, and when we realised that we had missed 'plumbing opportunities', we were allowed to nip back through immigration without even flashing a passport.

We were met outside the terminal by the spectacle of many bronzed knees, black socks, highly polished shoes and smiling faces. Everybody on official business wears the national dress that dates from the seventeenth century: for men, this means a *gho* or ankle-length coat hitched to the knee and neatly belted to form a pouch once used for daggers and food bowls, now for mobile phones, wallets and sometimes betel nuts. Each guide and driver wore a white silk scarf or *kabney* loosely from left shoulder to right hip. Sonam, our guide, and Gudu, our driver, produced *kabney* for us, to welcome us to Bhutan.

The first hours together as part of a team that will go through unpredictable, potentially dangerous experiences – often far from four-wheel drive or helicopter rescue – are always telling. Once we reached Thimpu, the capital, via an impressive though short dual carriageway whose central reservation was littered with sleeping dogs, Sonam was not alone in his relief that none of us took up his offer of a rest. Having proved ourselves by enjoying generous helpings of hot green chillies in a cheese sauce (*ema-datse*) to spice up the lunch thought bland enough for the tourist palate, we hit the town.

Sonam and Gudu proudly showed us as much as they could, always amusing, amused and unhurrying. In the Textile Museum we watched brightly coloured silk thread metamorphose into beautiful cloth on traditional looms. We watched archers practising in the Changlimithang Stadium where the pennants still fluttered from the recent Seventh National Coronation Archery Championships. A cat snoozed by the door of one temple and we managed to dodge a bucket of water thrown from an upstairs window after some diligent floor washing. Long ranks of prayer wheels were gently turned as monks passed.

We joined the crowd circumambulating the National Memorial Chorten, built to commemorate the third king of Bhutan by his mother in 1974. The elderly sat in rows on the steps of associated temples turning their beads and wheels. Thousands of butter candles sputtered; monks collected fruit and packets of crisps and handed them on to the senior priests to be blessed and distributed.

At the two-storey covered market – one floor for local and one for imported produce – we tried to identify the dried fish from India, and marvelled at the infinite choice of joss-sticks, shiny walnuts, betel leaves and limes, and the discerning way the monks selected their blood-black sausages.

Visitors are encouraged to wear the local dress so Sonam took us to a *gho* and *kira* emporium patronised by the Bhutanese. Women wear ankle-length wrap-around skirts called kira with little jackets. Much trying on followed and a small crowd gathered to watch, enjoying our readiness to laugh at ourselves. Unwittingly I found a particular *gho* woven in favourite colours that I chose in preference to a *kira*. It turned out to be the uniform for boys in a local primary school – and it caused universal mirth to see a grey-haired granny wearing it.

That evening in the hotel, lit by candles as the power had failed, we dined and drank in our new clothes and were asked to hush by a table of Europeans. We had bonded. The trek augured well.

❁ ❁ ❁

The atmospheric conditions prevented our flying east, so the following day we faced a twelve-hour drive. This proved a huge bonus for us all except Gudu who had to negotiate the road, which was rarely tarmacked and largely still under construction, with landslips, huge rocks brought down by gelignite and men with flags blocking the way. We gained a view of Bhutan that would otherwise have been denied us; we could stop, look, admire, enquire, photograph, shop, refresh, refuel, snooze and laugh.

We crossed gorges, got a grip on the five symbols painted on buildings to protect against demons, saw yak meat in strips on racks and red chillies on roofs drying in the hot sun, and discouraged a group of opportunist monkeys from climbing aboard our minibus. Rice was harvested and threshed on the terraces and little round stacks with mandarin hats were made with the straw. A group of women were voluntarily filling in potholes in this, Bhutan's national east-west highway. We were cheerily greeted by an elderly man pummelling his laundry with bare feet on a rock in an icy stream. In the pitch dark, having snaked through woods up mountain tracks, our heads lolling against the windows, Gudu finally turned off the engine. We had arrived at our B&B a few miles from our horses in central Bhutan, northeast of Jakar.

The Bhutanese have long used horses as pack animals but there is no culture of riding them. Not only had the horses and their tack had to be sourced, but they had had to be broken in, and Sonam had to learn to ride. The trek had been his project and five years in the planning. Proudly he introduced us to our steeds and to Pema, who had built the timber hay byre and looked after them in the newly fenced mountain paddocks. Also a complete novice, he was a natural horseman.

The term 'horse' is generic. These were ponies: small, chunky, woolly. It seemed a big ask to expect them to carry us over the high surrounding ridges, but off we set, bearing in mind 'horses for courses' and taking care not to let our feet knock their knees. Zig-zagging the fairly benign mountain path, soon we were way above the valley floor, looking down on the specks of workers in fields. Then we passed over the shoulder of the mountain and the valley was out of sight. We were to spend the next five days above three thousand metres riding through pine forests, across summer pastures and through mountain villages. The ponies clambered over boulders left by raging torrents of snowmelt, large enough to scrape their stomachs. They lurched through bogs, scrambled up paths and slithered down rivulet beds. From time to time they would pause to look to pick their way but not once did they object or baulk. Sometimes we would dismount to relieve them of their burden or the risk of unbalancing them. We scrambled, they scrambled; we rode on.

The nights turned chilly and here and there in the blackness of the pines was a brilliant gash of autumnal scarlet and burgundy Virginia creeper hanging from a treetop. Much of the open pasture was dotted with little pink cotoneaster; the forest edge had blobs of orange berberis and the evilly thorned, silver-branched bramble leaves had turned gold.

We camped in the clouds with only the sound of ponies chomping and the campfire logs hissing belligerently in the mizzle. In the morning the clouds were below us and the sky above was blue and the sun hot. Loosing the ponies to make the steep descent without our weight, we walked down via the Kunzangdra Monastery founded in 1488. Perched perilously, a revered nest of bees protected its treasure buried inside the sheer rock face.

After one particularly gruelling climb through the forest where the air was challengingly thin, as we broke out of the trees to a welcome breeze and the promise of the next pass, a deep growl indicated the presence of a large bull. As we continued to climb, his cows and calves came into view along with a wisp of smoke and prayer flags, and as we reached the top a herder and two women were sitting round the fire with their dogs. The women kept their distance but he walked over, chiding the dogs for their half-hearted aggression, and exchanged news with Sonam. The flags sent continuous prayers – the reward for whoever had climbed so far and high to place them there.

Four tiny young monks met us a short distance from Padselling Monastery. Having inspected our cameras, they insisted on helping carry our rucksacks to our sleeping quarters, even though the youngest, probably four or five, was barely tall enough to lift one off the ground. The monastery had the atmosphere of a boarding school at half term with all the senior monks in Jakar for the festival and a handful of twenty-year-olds left in charge. In the morning, as the clouds below dispersed, they kicked a deflated football like brothers until one coerced the smaller ones into reluctantly sweeping the area with birch brooms.

With the sun on our backs, we rode through villages until we came to a wide, energetic river. The way across was by chain-link bridge and we had already learned that crossing them requires balance and resolve as they bounce underfoot. To ride ponies across between hundreds of flapping, coloured prayer flags would have been unthinkable anywhere else or with any other equines. Gently encouraged by Pema, one willing pony led and the others gingerly followed. The bridge bucked and bounced. The white waters far below us were too clearly visible through the chain links. The only thing was to concentrate on the other side; once reached, chilled beer was the best.

In one farmhouse two of us slept on mattresses in the family shrine. Every household has one and any available funds are spent augmenting it. Lying on the floor beneath the altar gave scope for inspecting things in a way that in normal circumstances one would feel was intrusive. In every home there were photographs of all the five kings who have ruled Bhutan since 1907 when they replaced the feudal war lords – from early photographs, small, sepia and grainy, to colour photographs of the present king and his shy young bride, always large and in pride of place.

Wherever we stayed we were welcomed with homemade *arra*, a sake-like spirit, delicious and smooth despite being in much re-used Coca-Cola bottles. In a farmhouse with the working loom under the external ladder stairs, and a calf tethered in the vegetable patch, the bashed bottle had the 'worm' at the bottom. The worm, called *Yartsa Goenbub*, is actually a fungus, and has been reinvigorating those who could afford it since Chinese emperors discovered its properties thousands of years ago. Now Bhutanese farmers living too high for rice farming are allowed to collect and export the worms. We divided the two inches of magic between eight of us and waited for we knew not what.

The final climb to the 3,597-metre Febila Pass took us into dark, eerily quiet woods. Only the sounds of water splashing over rocks and the squelch of the ponies' legs pulling from the mud would have broken the silence had not Sonam regularly let out a piercing yell. Hoping to catch a glimpse of any wildlife, I asked him why he did it. 'To keep the yeti away,' he replied. We hung prayer flags at the top and led the ponies down.

Back in civilization, showered and shampooed, we were asked about our trek by other travellers. We had seen glorious country, but best of all we had been welcomed as guests of the Bhutanese at home. We had shared their food, *arra* and the worm. 'You obviously have had such fun…. you're all laughing,' they said, enviously. We had, and we were. Too sad for goodbyes, we persuaded Sonam to plan another trek.

Born in 1945, **Sue Bathurst** studied painting and drawing in Marseille and London. She has worked in television; as a freelance journalist; as an historic property management consultant; and has farmed corn and sheep. Now, when not horse trekking, she runs a boutique B&B in Gloucestershire. She is widowed with one married son.

The Silver Steamers

Sarah Pope

'What was that?'

A bolt the size of a trombone dropped out of the upholstery and hit the floor, rolling to the rhythm of the pre-revolutionary observation carriage of the Trans-Caucasian Steam Express. It crisscrossed the starburst motifs baked into the linoleum, circled our flayed, moulting armchairs and ditched under the dinosaur TV cabinet. The TV faced outwards and was purely structural. It reinforced and blockaded the back door.

Five blasts on the whistle. Daniel stood up.

'Time for the run-past! Can you get some beers in, Gran?'

'What! You can't have got through that whole crate?'

'We used eight of them to flush the toilet, remember, and the last three to clean the footplate.'

I glanced down the line. We were making a dash for the North Caucasus freight depot at Mineralnye Vody to fit in a photoshoot before dark.

Daniel had been an infant entrepreneur. We only found out he was selling his school lunches to buy train miles when the stationmaster phoned from Sheffield to say, 'Your little boy is asking passengers for pocket money in return for help with their timetables. We think he should be in school.'

Now he's a teenager selling 'Rare Track Travel' to mature trainspotters. I was flattered when he asked me to come along for the ride.

'You'd like it, Gran. It's a seniors rail club this time – The Silver Steamers. They're all your age. Mum says you need a break.'

The Silver Steamers were already bursting into the observation car with long lenses, anxious not to miss a coupling. The blue-and-gold-liveried P36 Express loco, number 0218, straight out of *Thomas the Tank Engine*, gleamed on the turntable, the catwalk of the Caucasus, surrounded by a field of derelict diesel hulks, filthy grey, with smashed windows.

'First Sitting Stan' from Oldham was in the lead as you'd expect.

'Is your Daniel about?' he asked, forcing his way to the window. 'Only I could do with the second sitting tonight, what with this run-past.'

'So could we all, Stan, so could we all…' Engineer Lawrence, a genuine railwayman, retired, from the Crewe depot, pulled rank on trainspotter Stan, the amateur 'gricer'. He made a point of tightening a few nuts on the viewing bench as he came through, obstructing Stan's progress.

Daniel climbed onto the bench with a nod to Lawrence.

'A moment of your time, gentlemen, before we stop for the Mineralnye Vody run-past. Don't worry, you won't miss supper. It's been put back an hour and a half tonight. Supper 9 p.m. tonight.'

There was a shocked murmur from the floor.

'What did he say? Changed the timetable? Make sure you get the first sitting tonight, Len, to go with your medication, or it'll be too late…'

A warm front of boiling cabbage drifted from the galley at the business end. The chef was getting up steam regardless.

I knew what I had to do. As we slowed into the siding, hooting and grinding, people appeared, running alongside. Dogs ran to and fro, barking, under the moving train. I started my weary window shutter workout. Bend, grab, heave, hook. Better than physio for my wonky knee. Our babushka, Irina, from the rear samovar, looked in to check on the deal we had made.

At Rostov-on-Don, the start of our journey, Irina had insisted we must proceed, day and night, with the shutters on every window closed to discourage target practice along the tracks.

'Do something, Granny,' said Daniel, 'or we're out of business. This is a sightseeing tour!'

So I plied Irina with whisky miniatures for three days and she began to see how reliable I was. Every morning I walked the train with her, unhanging shutters. Every evening or halt she let me walk the train on my own, rehanging shutters. I wasn't going to lose a window.

Now and then, Irina invited me into her kiosk where she kept control of the water and power supplies and an emergency twenty-foot ladder, locked to the samovar. She propped the door open with an axe and trickled us a cuppa.

Babushka Ludmilla at the dormitory end of the train was easier. She showed me how Cossacks open vodka bottles with their wedding rings, helped with the shutter walk at night and supervised the rubbish bucket, padlocked on top of her samovar. Her business plan was reclaiming deposits on beer bottles. Whenever I passed by, she unlocked the bucket for extra seating and shared a tipple.

A final jolt and we had stopped for the engine change. Lawrence and Stan staggered off the high step with their tripods, aiming for best shot at the glorious P36 before it coupled to the front of the train, along with two good compartments specially selected and cleaned for the photoshoot. The back end stayed on the main line under babushka control.

The rest of the Silver Steamers jostled into position for an hour and a half of 'run-pasts' in the siding – all that shunting to and fro while the photographers stood in each other's way, tearful from smuts, sharing the driver's tea straight from the boiler and waiting for that perfect, photogenic curl of vapour.

Ludmilla took my arm and swung me off the rear step, clear of the line. The tracks were loaded with decades of dog and human dirt. Now and then, the wheels squirted a blend of fine noxious mud at the Silver Steamers.

The pop-up market arrived, parading up and down the tracks like a chorus line selling souvenirs – especially local railway signboards and icons. An old man, dragging a sack of tools, surveyed the train for broken windows, offering to make instant repairs with duct tape. Irina defended her doorway, leaning on the axe, frowning.

'Piva! Piva!' I practised my word aloud, hoping it meant the right sort of beer, and shook my head at the smiling girl who approached, head in a fuzzy shawl, offering a tray of coffee glasses docked in wet sand.

'Niet. Piva!' I said, but she handed me a glass anyway, grinning a mouthful of wrecked teeth.

'What is your name?' she practised saying. 'My name is Cora.'

I walked the line for beer. Every ten yards or so, a group of boys manned trestle tables stocked with a few cloudy bottles, more or less filled. They shook a bottle overhead now and then to attract attention.

Cardboard signs in English said: 'Buy 30 rouble', and further down the track, 'Buy 28 rouble', 'Buy 25 rouble', 'Buy 24 rouble' – all written in the same hand.

From previous experience, we were counting on four 'drinkers' to every eight 'flushers' we purchased. You couldn't tell, they all looked the same, so I chose a couple of bottles from each table down the line, to hedge our bets. When the trolley was full, I offered thirty roubles a bottle all round, no complications.

Wrong. A frightful banging on tables meant I was undermining the pricing code and the capitalist social order.

A very small boy staggered in front of me, dragging a bag of blistered tomatoes. He blew the smoke of a pretend cigarette over me as I chose. When I handed over my king-size duty frees, his accomplice rolled a watermelon towards my feet.

The loco whistle sounded for departure. Most of us were back on board, sprucing up for the evening meal. I was very grateful for the stop at Mineralnye Vody; the name translates as 'mineral water' and it is, unsurprisingly, a spa town, where the water tanks could be topped up. Lev's restaurant car and the steam locos were entitled to first call on the water supply, which usually left a rusty trickle for the trough in the communal washroom compartment. Now and then, Irina, at plumbing control, took pity and diverted the supply to us. Ludmilla kindly stood watch at the washroom door when I seized the chance of a semi-strip wash. We all ignored the corroded showerhead in the corner, currently used to secure an obsolete piece of telegraphic equipment.

Daniel's voice came over the intercom: 'Will Mr Stan Powell and Mr Lawrence Bowden please come to the restaurant car when they are back on board.'

They didn't come.

'What shall we do, Gran? They're not on board. How could we lose them at a run-past?'

We had an hour to spare. Then we would forfeit our departure slot. It was single track after this. No chance to make up time on our speed limit.

I talked to a few of the passengers in the second sitting. They looked up, grudging, from their meat hash. No, they hadn't seen Stan, or Lawrence, for that matter. But those two wouldn't be together, would they? Chalk and cheese. Try the footplate.

Instead, I tried the Miss Marple approach. Motive? If I was a Silver Steamer, what could possibly persuade me to abandon a run-past in company with my keenest rival?

Of course – a decent beer.

And there was the Hotel Mineralnye Vody in full view, a few hundred yards the wrong side of the tracks.

'Go, Granny, go!' said Daniel. 'If you're not back in fifteen, I'll come and get you.'

I borrowed a torch and a walking stick from the luggage rack and backed down the steps, bad knee first.

The pop-up market had dematerialised. A skinny dog followed me out of the railway yard. It sat down and howled when I showed it my walking stick. I headed slowly for the dim lights of the hotel through a hole in the fence.

There was no sign of Lawrence or Stan in the bar, but there was a restaurant advertised on the fourth floor. I found the lift, which went down instead of up. At lower ground level, the doors opened and there they were, Stan and Lawrence, framed in a small glass foyer. I stepped out of the lift.

'Keep hold of the lift!'

'No problem, Mr Powell.' I recalled the lift.

A moment later the doors opened.

'Press four, press four!' Stan shouted.

'Don't let them in!' Lawrence shouted.

Up one floor, the doors opened and three more people joined us. The overload alarm sounded.

'I'm not getting out this time,' said Lawrence as we returned to Lower Ground. But the three locals pushed us out like cuckoos emptying a nest.

'That's the third time and counting,' said Lawrence.

Through the glass, we could see hotel staff moving about with mops and buckets in the spa water tasting hall. We banged on the glass and they ignored us. Another four people were pushed out of the lift into our foyer. We all shouted and thumped on the glass.

Next lift, Daniel was pushed out to join us, with a few more victims. The little foyer was filling up with panic-stricken tourists seeking the restaurant. Most of them were still smoking their duty-frees. It was very stuffy and hard to breathe.

'Daniel! Thank the Lord! So get us out of this one!'

Stan was abnormally red and breathing hard, leaning on a wooden ashtray built like a bird table. Lawrence was holding Stan's bag for him as a one-off concession.

Daniel burrowed through the crush, uncoupled the ashtray from Stan, raised it above his head and performed a perfectly judged back foot leg glance at the glass door into the spa hall. The concussion produced a pile of shards. We picked our way over the wreckage. Nobody took any notice.

It was getting dark when we found the hole in the depot fence. There were spurts of flame and urgent hooting from the Caucasian

Express. She was getting up steam, now headed by two bullish L class 2-10-10s, ready for the challenging gradient into Kislovodsk.

I was mortified for Daniel. Stan and Lawrence, his most demanding clients, had just missed a double engine change.

Spattered in smuts, they manhandled me up the steps of the washroom carriage. We knew the lock was broken on that door. We were in.

No sign of the babushkas and no lights, to deter snipers. My foot caught on something in the doorway and I hurtled into the middle of a game of skittles set up in the observation car. Irina's tripwire. I should have known! To foil intruders when she was off-duty. I jogged the bowler's elbow as I fell, and precipitated his throw. All ten beer bottles went down with one swipe of the melon. The ripe and ready grenade burst open, hurling pips and pulp all over the carriage.

'A strike! A strike!' The players stood up as one and applauded.

Ludmilla loomed over me, wringing her hands and returning my spectacles.

'Vodka,' she concluded, checking my pulse.

Irina passed the bottle.

Sarah Pope has travelled the world as a viola player and is just back from working with her string quartet on a Saga cruise in the Mediterranean. She has written a violin book for beginners (*A New Tune a Day*) and enjoys teaching late starter adults the fun of music.

Across the Desert on Camelback

Robert Spence

The total age of the four of us was two hundred and fifty, and that included Jon who'd not reached forty. We were setting off to retrace the 176 miles across the Bayuda Desert in Sudan crossed by the Relief Expedition in 1885, sent to attempt to rescue General Gordon from Khartoum. But I, as leader, was more than a little nonplussed when our chief camel driver, Bala, said he had never *heard* of our first destination, Jakdul Wells – the staging post used by the British army on that march.

'Is there water there?' he asked me through Jon, our Arabic speaker.

'Oh yes,' I replied. I knew there had been plenty in 1885 – but well into the twenty-first century, with five days of travel for the camels to reach the oasis, I dared not consider that it might now be dry. Jakdul Wells was the place I had dreamed of reaching during those months of planning this trip, and there was no way I was going to agree to cross the desert by the westerly and quite different route that our camel driver knew.

It had taken eighteen months to plan, researching the route with regimental museums whose soldiers had taken part, reading every available book on Gordon and his history and – not least – persuading three friends to come with me. None of us had ridden a camel, but one had been a master of foxhounds, another a New Zealand sheep farmer, used to riding over the hills. My own experience had been in hill trekking, mostly on foot; and Jon, half our age, was an Arabic-speaking diplomat. I decided we had to follow the army's route backwards – it was too difficult to arrange for camels to start from the small Nile-side town of Korti, as the army had done to shortcut across the huge bulge in the river. Getting our visas was extremely uncertain, but with only three weeks before we hoped to set off – in the short window between chilly winter and scorching summer – George, the local hotelier and 'Mister Fix-it' in Khartoum, was able to email us the long-awaited paperwork, and we managed to get on to a flight.

After the flurry of arrival usual at any Third World airport, George's driver met us and we were introduced to our cook, Montessir, recommended by the experienced Sahara traveller Michael Asher, and we accompanied Montessir round markets as he stocked up on provisions. George had arranged for the camels and crew to meet us at Metemma, a small town about eighty miles north of Khartoum, which was where the original desert column had reached the Nile again on their way from Korti. The next morning we loaded up with all the camping gear and food and set off up the east side of the river in two 4-wheel-drive vehicles – one of which broke down on the way, so we spent the night on a patch of sand without most of our bedding or food, as our lead vehicle went to rescue the other. I slept in my clothes underneath a spare mattress, in the absence of a sleeping bag.

After that very chilly night we crossed the Nile on a local ferry, hoping to set off on the camels from the far bank. But we had not reckoned with a fierce and unseasonal sandstorm that blew for the next twenty-four hours. It was then I learned from Bala that he had not heard of Jakdul Wells. Realising we had to find our own route, we produced our GPS and the only map we had managed to acquire, an aerial one prepared for small aircraft. We said farewell to the cars and set off into the teeth of the sandstorm next day, each of us perched uncomfortably on top of a baggage-laden camel, and covered a long twenty-eight miles. Each time we stopped to check our position we found that Bala had veered off west towards the well that he knew and we had to persuade him to turn north again.

I love the desert. Many people think it must be dull and all the same, but the scenery varies from stony ground to high sand dunes to scrubby areas where camels can snatch a passing mouthful. For four days we travelled on, the camels picking their way to avoid stones. I wasn't sleeping well, worried about the very real possibility that Jakdul would be dry. But on the fifth day we could see the high cliffs behind a barren rocky basin where the army had made camp. And to my relief we found tracks of goats heading in that direction – the first sign of any other life since we had left the Nile.

Bala waved us ahead on foot, urging us to find the water, and sure enough as we rounded the rocks we could see a green and stagnant pool. What a relief! In fact there were three pools on different levels in the rocks. The camels enjoyed a good drink at the first one and after they had had their fill, Bala filled up our jerrycans from the same green water. Well-laced with a double dose of iodine, we found it not unpalatable, though I have tasted better!

Sadly we had only time to spend one day at Jakdul to look over the broken-down fortifications made so long ago by those squaddies so far from home. Then it was back onto the camels for five more days. A medieval scene at a remote desert well 180 feet deep, where goat skins were still used to raise the water, gave a glimpse of the very hard life nomads still lead.

At last we reached Korti and were able to unfold our weary, stiff legs from the wooden camel saddles. It was the end of a memorable and unique journey – not done, we believe, on camelback by any other traveller for over one hundred and twenty-five years.

Robert Spence is a retired chartered civil engineer, born in 1935, living in Hertfordshire. Educated at Rugby School and Imperial College, he is married with two daughters and four grandchildren. After retirement he trekked in mountains and deserts and is a fellow of The Royal Geographical Society.

The Bishop's Cloak
Pamela Hardyment

Bullets whizzed past my ears amid the burning tyres and teargas of a West Bank demonstration near Jerusalem. I never imagined that after a lifetime sitting at a desk in various book publishing houses, and now comfortably retired, I would suddenly get up at sixty-six and find myself in the Middle East, hanging on for dear life to an ancestral cross.

As I got used to afternoon naps and long days in front of the computer in the suburbs of London, I had become an armchair observer of events throughout the Middle East, a Facebook devotee. A life-altering event, the death of my Swiss partner, brought about unimaginable changes to what I once considered a certain future of gentle swimming and bridge. I began to do all those things that are left to a grieving relative, giving away clothes and sorting through letters and papers, seeing things I had not looked at for many years.

One day, I took out of a drawer the ancient clothes and personal items of my partner's great-great-great-grandfather, a certain Bishop Gobat of Jerusalem, which were now mine for safekeeping. With my new yearning to do something else in life, alone, I became more interested in the history behind the heavy black cloak, which reached to my knees, with its red, embroidered lapel and delicate white gauze scarf; the fine jewel-encrusted dagger which undoubtedly had protected the bishop during turbulent years in the mid nineteenth century in the Old City of Jerusalem; the double inkwell he would have used daily to write his memoirs of his missionary days in Abyssinia, Malta and the Holy Land.

Samuel Gobat was a Swiss Anglican Bishop born in the Jura in 1799. His ministry in the Old City of Jerusalem lasted for thirty-three years and it was his last resting place. I had two portraits in small oval frames from those years: one of him, a large, bearded, strong-looking man, and one of his stout Swiss wife; plus a beautiful German print of Omar's Mosque in Jerusalem, made in the nineteenth century, which had always watched over me in my home office. The usual internecine arguments among the varied protestant sections of Jerusalem evangelical life, especially among the English and German communities over which he ministered, must have turned his thoughts to another project that would have lasting value. Just outside the Old City by the Jaffa Gate, not far from his own home, he built a school for orphaned Arabs and the elite of Palestine who would later become politicians and doctors. The beautiful school with its famous Protestant Cemetery was, I discovered thanks to the internet, still there and operating as an American College.

. Here was the sign for me to get on the road. I would give all these precious historical items back to the college the bishop had created.

Leaving Jordan's capital of Amman, I arrived at the Allenby Crossing to face the lengthy questions of the Israeli border guards. I was wearing the large, elaborate, hand-forged silver cross I had found among my partner's possessions. I thought of the bishop.

'What is the purpose of your visit?' the young man asked.

'I have come to deliver the bishop's cloak, and to pray,' I said. Little did I know then what I was to suffer later, and that I would be on my knees praying for my life.

I wanted to experience Jerusalem and the Old City straight away. I was struck dumb, and in tears, by the view from my hotel of the Dome of the Rock on a warm, blue, starlit night. It was beyond my wildest spiritual dreams. I was back in history seeing what the bishop saw every day from the rooftop of his house, the beautiful Mount Zion and the hills of Palestine. I visited the college, outside the Old City down a dusty road, and found it intact and as delightful as in the prints I had seen in the bishop's memoirs. His substantial tomb, with a relief of his head and carvings in marble, was guarded by iron railings and a gnarled, overhanging olive tree, all still pitted with bullets from the days of the Ottoman Empire.

After delivering the clothes to a delighted principal and enjoying the complex with its magnificent gardens overlooking Mount Zion, I moved on and caught a bus heading towards Bethlehem. I arrived at a camp where a good friend of mine was living. Dheisheh was one of the first refugee camps to be created in 1948, but nothing had prepared me for the starkness, the poverty and the sense of impermanence of a place which had existed for sixty-five years. My friend, who was originally from Haifa, showed me the one room where his family of ten were housed as they fled those who had come to take over his land back in 1948. Here in the camp there were no gardens, but a mass of purple bougainvillea and heavily scented white jasmine overhanging small plots of vegetables.

'Why are there no gardens?' I asked.

'We do not want to make this permanent, our home is in Haifa. We will return.'

My friend gave me the address of a women's peace house near Nablus which he thought I would like to visit. It was a small village, dusty, with overflowing garbage bins and dozens of feral cats, small whitewashed houses and exquisite gardens filled with orange and lemon trees, great bushes of fiery red azaleas and row upon row of vegetables. I joined an American, an Irishwoman and a German in the large house with its courtyard shaded by vines and apricot trees. I was glad to be in this beautiful country, feeling strong and well. I never told the younger women at the peace house my real age, and I had to act as if I had no fear.

One Friday, after a delicious lunch of homemade hummus, tomatoes from the vine and apricots from the garden, with fresh bread as large as a bicycle wheel made by Fatima in the house alongside ours, we set off for Qalandiya, near Jerusalem. The taxi drove through acres and acres of silver-leaved olive groves, a beautiful sight as the trees were bending with their autumn fruit ripe for shaking and picking. On arrival at the central dual carriageway, the smell of Arabic coffee and cooking falafel made us stop for yet another taste of Palestine. The smoke in the distance made us a little nervous.

'Oh, that's normal, it happens every Friday after prayers,' said one of the boys serving us, his Palestinian red and white scarf tied tightly around his head and trailing down his back.

We joined the throng of people heading towards the smoke. Flags were flying, red and black and green. Young men and women joined hands. Some of the protestors were my age, singing and chanting for their freedom, and I joined in heartily.

'Don't go to the barriers, my dear,' said the knowledgeable American lady, 'just stick with us.'

I had no fear, I was excited; I went to the barrier and started to take photographs. Suddenly everybody started running back and I was alone.

'Come on lady!' shouted a young Palestinian, and then the tear gas surrounded me.

I could not breathe and fell to my knees, staring at the dusty ground, throwing up and unable to see clearly. I felt for my cross.

'Come on, get out of here, those are real bullets!' shouted a young man who dragged me by the arms as shells whizzed past and pinged on the drainpipes and windows of the buildings. He threw me onto the ground in an empty shop.

I had learnt my lesson, but I went back again the next week. I realised that I must follow my conscience and the ladies from the peace house and do what I came to do. We worked together and forged fabulous friendships. It was, however, with some relief that I booked into my hotel in Jericho for the final leg of the journey home. I was anxious to make my plane the next morning and be back in the safety of England, and to see my family again. I had to be at my eldest son's wedding in three days' time.

The hotel was in a camp, and as I realised that the falafel sandwich I had eaten earlier in the day was probably home to several flies before, I summoned every ounce of strength to get to the bathroom and back. I finally fell asleep in the empty hotel, to be woken by the metallic ping of bullets ricocheting off the metal shopfront downstairs where I had earlier taken my mint tea. It was three in the morning. I wanted to go out and take photographs. Luckily I could not get up as my stomach burned and churned. The next morning as I left, I noticed that the bullet holes were close to the front door I would have exited had I been fit and well in the night. I longed for England.

I made my son's wedding, though I was looking shattered. My children, now fathers themselves and keen to have at least one grandma still alive to play a part in their children's lives, suggested I shouldn't go back to the West Bank.

But I was hooked, and I returned and helped in the peace house again and to this day I have absolutely no regrets. In fact, I am planning my next trip right now. Sorry, boys. Last time I travelled to Palestine, I saw the special glass case which now housed all the things which had drawn me to Jerusalem in the first place. The principal of the American University College had built the splendid vitrine, and even copied the emblem of the bishop's hat from the tomb, while he was resting from a heart operation.

'Your precious things helped me recover,' he said.

Pamela Hardyment lives in London and studied modern languages at university before taking up a career in journalism and book publishing. Her translation from the German of Tadeus Pfeifer's poetry, *The Basalt Womb*, was published in 2004 by Jay Landesman Publishers, London. *Dancing Alone*, a collection of her poems, was published by von Loeper Verlag in 2005.

Return to Kiev

Katheryn Stavrakis Lesley

I came to Kiev, alone, on the first anniversary of my mother's death. Ukraine in October 2014 was not an obvious travel choice for a sixty-two-year-old woman. Earlier that year the Euromaidan revolution had taken place, the president fled to Russia, and war still raged in the eastern part of the country; in July, a Malaysia Airlines passenger plane was shot down.

It was my third trip to Kiev, but my only solo one. In 1995, shortly after the fall of communism, my parents and I had made the trip, their only visit to their homeland since fleeing during the Second World War. Nearly twenty years later, in the summer of 2013, I had fulfilled a long-held dream and brought my two daughters to Ukraine to see where their grandparents and many ancestors, *predki*, came from. Kiev seemed lively and flourishing, light years away from 1995; we could not have predicted the bloody and dangerous turn of events that was to follow only months later.

But I knew I would go back. For me, understanding my past has not been a simple matter of genealogy or visits to hometowns where old timers would remember us. I grew up in the United States during the Cold War. My family's country of origin was behind the Iron Curtain; history remained sealed in archives and travel was not generally permitted. Letters from relatives arrived months after being posted, crudely ripped open and re-taped. There was misinformation coming from all directions.

We were astonished at the rapid crumbling of the Soviet Union in 1991. It had seemed impenetrable, a monument for the ages, yet suddenly nothing remained. One of the most powerful governments on earth had not even outlasted my father, who was born into the fray in 1917.

In the past twenty years, a flood of new information has emerged, and with the internet there is more available than ever before. Using Google Maps I could look up the very streets where my parents lived – something none of us could have envisioned when I was younger. And travel has, of course, become possible. I was gripped with excitement. I wanted to breathe the same air my parents had; see what they had described to me in many stories, understand their lives from the inside. And I could finally do so.

Very few people knew of my plans. I didn't want to explain myself – in fact, I couldn't. I am a cautious person by nature and have no desire to put myself in danger simply for risk's sake. When in 2014 the political situation intensified, I watched the news, corresponded with people, and weighed the possibilities, finally deciding that if I stayed in Kiev and possibly Western Ukraine, the risks would not be too great. I had been corresponding with a historian, Vitaliy, who would serve as a contact, and had spent a year relearning Russian, my first language, just barely holding my own in a classroom of very bright twenty-year-olds. (My mother spoke Ukrainian as well, but Russian was the language of the home. I am keenly aware of the political implications, but there was no time for me to learn a new tongue.)

Not being a young traveller anymore, I planned carefully. I wanted to blend in as much as possible to avoid becoming a target, so I bypassed areas tourists preferred, and where locals always seemed eager to steer me, assuming my preferences as an American. From my last visit I knew of a comfortable, inexpensive guesthouse in a residential area of Kiev, only a couple of metro stops from the centre. It was just as I had remembered, except for one glaring difference: a year before it had housed visitors on holiday or business from various parts of Ukraine, Russia and some European cities; now many rooms were taken by refugees fleeing the violence in the east, or more accurately, as the receptionist Anna explained to me, those who could afford to flee.

⊕ ⊕ ⊕

On a lovely day in October 2014, with the shadows of leaves from ancient horse chestnut trees flickering on the cobblestones, I stood diagonally across the narrow roadway from my great-grandfather's mansion on Malopodvalnaya Street in Kiev's historic upper city. My mother's grandfather, born a serf, had worked his way to prominence as a businessman and member of the *duma*. He owned a crystal shop in the city centre. In the early twentieth century, he built the house for his wife Yelena and their four children, including my grandmother Anna. 'It was a huge mansion,' my mother had told me, drawing sketches on napkins at the kitchen table. 'It covered a whole city block in the centre of Kiev.' But with the self-centredness of youth, only half-listening, I didn't really believe her until I saw it for myself.

With its ornate exterior and tall windows, the house was much as she had described it, although it had been converted into expensive condominiums and boxy balconies now marred its façade. The street was famous enough that Mikhail Bulgakov, the early-twentieth-century author famous for *The Master and Margarita*, even used it in his novel *The White Guard*. My family's fortunes changed in 1918, the year my mother was born, as the Russian Revolution took hold and

Kiev was thrown into chaos. Private property was seized. The house was turned into a *kommunalka*, communal apartments, and people from all over the country were crammed into any available spaces, cooking on hotplates in hallways and washing dishes in bathrooms. My great-grandfather died of a stroke, and my great-grandmother Yelena, my grandparents and my infant mother, after first fleeing the city for a village, cautiously returned some months later and were allotted one room for all of them, later expanded to two.

On this autumn day, I looked straight across the intersection to the corner room my mother had shared with her grandmother Yelena, once mistress of the house. During our trip here in 1995, on the night we arrived, my parents and I walked through the streets of Kiev. In the soft misty rain, my father said he had the odd feeling that time had vanished and he didn't know where he was, or when. Where was his home? Here in Kiev or in the US? As we rounded a corner the house on Malopodvalnaya, then being remodelled, emerged from the darkness in a glow of streetlights. It seemed as if we could walk right in and our people would be going about their lives, ready to offer us tea and sweets.

Now, standing there on my own, both my parents gone, I imagined my mother as I had seen her in a photo taken in that same room while she recovered from scarlet fever. She leaned against the dark wooden backboard of the bed, an extraordinarily beautiful girl of about fourteen, hair parted on one side, falling across her face and framing her high cheekbones. There is a porch in front of that entrance, and I have a black and white photo of my mother sitting on it wearing a cotton print dress, knees hugged to her chest, her spaniel Topsic by her side. She looks up from beneath the wave of her hair into the camera with a direct gaze that's both startling and confrontational, like a dare; locking eyes with the observer, yet also seeing beyond into some mysterious, distant future. Almost exactly a year ago to the day, I saw the same look as my mother lay dying, a world and lifetime away in Portland, Oregon. Holding her hand, I leaned in close and her gaze locked mine for a long moment, still mysterious, but with a sadness more profound than any I had seen before. I knew she was saying goodbye.

Across the street from the house on Malopodvalnaya, to my left, was a grey stone office building which had been the Central Office of the feared NKVD, called KGB in English, and which now still serves as headquarters of the Ukrainian Security Services. Through my internet searches I discovered that when my family lived there in the 1930s, the agency was run by Lavrenti Beria, one of Stalin's notorious henchmen. In an ironic twist, Baba Lena, as my mother called her grandmother, was one of the *bivshiye lyudi*, or 'former people', who were to be exterminated by the new Soviet world order. She lived pretty much hidden in the room of her former home, trying, I imagine, to avoid drawing attention to herself and her family. My mother adored her, and described her as a gentle and loving woman, without a trace of anger or bitterness. In the few remaining photos I have seen, her kind eyes bear this out.

That room was now an office, and it was late afternoon. As I watched, a pale young woman stepped out onto the porch, smoking and nervously checking her mobile phone, evidently waiting for a ride. On the other side of the house, facing the Secret Service headquarters, cars were parked along the narrow street, brand new and expensive-looking. A long black Range Rover with tinted windows pulled up and waited, engine idling, until a girl of about ten wearing the checked skirt and knee socks of a private school uniform skipped across the street to let herself in, blond ponytail swinging behind her. The SUV pulled away and I was struck by the irony that, at one time, the appearance of a long black car with tinted windows would have been terrifying: these cars had a nickname, *chorni voron*, 'black crow', and were used by the secret police to arrest people, usually in the middle of the night.

But right then, in the golden light of an autumn afternoon, I was taken back a hundred years to imagine my grandmother as a girl, running down the front steps every Sunday at that very same spot to a waiting carriage, possibly also with her blond hair streaming behind her, on her way to the bakery with her father for *rosachki*. Ukraine astonished me not with how much had changed, but with what remained; if I squinted my eyes a bit, it looked just as it must have long ago.

A few blocks further along I reached a massive plaza bookended by the famous Saint Sophia's Cathedral, a UNESCO World Heritage Site, where my grandmother Anna was married, and directly across from it the breathtaking Saint Michael's Golden-Domed Cathedral, destroyed by the Soviet government in the 1930s and rebuilt in 1999. My historian friend showed me architectural plans from that era: both churches were meant to be razed and replaced by hundred-foot -tall statues of Lenin. A group of professors and architects had been called in to verify that these priceless structures had no real artistic or historical value and could therefore justifiably be destroyed, and they all did so, but one. The holdout who objected was thrown into prison and died there.

I followed the street to Maidan Nezalezhnosti, or Independence Square, where the recent protests had taken place. Along the side of the square were memorials to the 'Heavenly Hundred', people killed during that time, a number of them by a hail of sniper fire from tall buildings in February 2014. There were photographs of the victims decorated with religious symbols and objects from their lives: a worn shoe, books, inscribed photos of loved ones, helmets, notes to the deceased. They were men, women, young, old, smiling, serious. I came upon a patch of land surrounded by chicken wire and in the centre a photo of a boy's face, not more than eighteen years old. A woman kneeled, digging out weeds and grass with her hands. I noticed she was weeding the same spot, over and over again. She was the right age to be the boy's mother. Next to her stood a man who could have been his father, hands in his pockets, staring into the distance.

Overlooking the square, a small wooden chapel had been built. I pulled on the scarf that I kept in my bag for such occasions and entered. Several people stood before the lit icon. One woman cried in silence, not bothering to wipe away the tears.

I came to Kiev to honour my mother and my *predki*; it's a long trip from Oregon, and I don't bounce back as well as I once did. But I am deeply grateful that I've lived long enough for this trip to become a reality. And I know I need to return to Ukraine.

Katheryn Stavrakis Lesley is a writer and editor, the first in her family born in the United States. The fall of the Soviet Union has given her the opportunity to understand her parents' country of birth. She lives in Portland, Oregon with her husband, the author Craig Lesley, and has two daughters.

Close Encounters with Local Cultures

The Train from Havana

Dervla Murphy

In 2005 Dervla Murphy travelled in Cuba with her daughter and three grandchildren, returning the following year at the age of seventy-four to travel in her own style, a combination of hitchhiking, walking and public transport.

Undaunted by previous experience, I booked a seat on the twice-weekly Havana-Bayamo train service (alleged dep. 7.25 p.m.). The only alternatives were hitchhiking, which could take several days, or a Viazul coach.

At 8.50 p.m. we passengers were loosed onto the ill-lit platform and confusion immediately set in; even by daylight the faint print on my ticket, giving coach, compartment and seat numbers, was well nigh illegible. When I opened a coach door at random its inner panel fell off, blocking my way. Clambering over it, I groped down a corridor by a glimmer of platform light and found an empty compartment where I was still alone at 9.45. The engine then made eerie noises, setting it apart from any other engine I've known, and moved off at a slow walking speed. All this seemed too good to be true; silence and darkness blessed my coach, whatever its number: I could stretch out and sleep, at least until the first stop.

Some time later three chain-smoking adults and a fretful

toddler woke me. Unsurprised, I sat up, eyelids drooping, and tried to determine from the voices how many of each sex were present; for moments the toddler was so fretful I thought she/he (?) was two toddlers. Soon the adults (two male, one female) were furiously quarrelling and exhaling rum fumes. Cubans tend to shout, even when not arguing, possibly because conversations must often compete with insanely amplified music coming from several different directions. This row, inexplicably, quieted the toddler.

An hour or so later, when the last cigarettes had been stamped on the floor and everyone except me was asleep, all hell broke loose nearby. A conductress was on the prowl, checking everyone's seating. In Havana, where conflicting views were held about the numbering of twelve unmarked coaches, many passengers had settled wherever they could find space and now resented being moved. Oddly enough, my companions were correctly placed – very clever of them, I thought. Now the combination of her own dying torch and my faintly inked ticket challenged our conductress. Only when one of the men lent his cigarette-lighter could she see that mine was seat three in compartment B in coach six – three coaches away. She then recruited this same man to lead me through total darkness. He wore my rucksack, I carried my shoulder-bag and used my umbrella to steady myself: hereabouts the train was behaving like a small boat on a stormy sea.

One is accustomed to the bits between coaches moving beneath one's feet – that's unalarming. In this case however there were no bits: one had to leap from coach to coach. As we moved slowly along the corridor of the second coach I felt the floor giving beneath my feet and momentarily I panicked. However, the sinking floor sensation happened repeatedly and was just another of the Bayamo service's idiosyncrasies and not immediately threatening – though one day those rotting boards may well claim victims.

In coach number six my guide used his cigarette-lighter to peer at labels, then roused a man comfortably curled up on two seats – his and mine, apparently. Without complaint, he shifted his position as I thanked my guide; until then, he and I had exchanged not a word. With rucksack on lap, because I couldn't see where to store it, I leant back in my seat and received a small but painful scalp wound; it oozed enough blood to matt my hair. Where a headrest had been three sharp metal spikes protruded. My bag contained one tin of Buccanero, for emergencies. I now felt its time had come and quickly drank it – a mistake...

In due course those 355ml sought the exit and by the light of a full moon, newly emerged from dispersing clouds, I located the *baño* – seemingly occupied. Having waited a reasonable time I tried the door again, pushing hard. It swung open to reveal a vacuum: below was Mother Earth. At a certain point one ceases to believe in the reality of what's happening – it must all be an illusion – yet somehow one has to go along with it. But for the moon, I would have stepped forward to my death – not exactly a premature death but an unpleasant and rather silly way to go. The door bore a prominent notice – DANGER! DO NOT OPEN! – but some more drastic deterrent is required in an unlit train that habitually travels by night. Opposite the *baño* was the coach exit, its steps conveniently missing so that one could pee, more or less accurately, onto the track. But only more or less: such situations provoke penis envy.

The *baño* at the other end of number six, visited during the day, had no door – or loo or washbasin, though their sites were obvious. Here one had to relieve one's bladder and bowels in full view of passers-by. The latter activity was performed as close as possible to the walls – a much used space, halfway through our twenty-hour journey.

We covered the first two hundred and fifty miles in eleven-and-a-half hours including a long stop in Santa Clara, while a passenger train and two freight trains passed on their way to Havana. Then, speeding up, we achieved fifty miles in one-and-a-half hours. After that I lost interest in our progress and concentrated on my awakening companions. All five were going to a conference at Bayamo University and their company made the travail of moving to coach six seem worthwhile. Four spoke English – 'necessary for our research'. Academic salaries left them with no choice but to take this unbelievable train, one-third the price of the cheapest bus. My tourist ticket cost CP25.50, they paid the equivalent of CP1.50.

From Bayamo's station a ten-minute walk took me to Miranda's rather luxurious *casa particular* where my hostess exclaimed, '*Desde Havana el tren! Muy dificil!*' '*Si,*' I agreed, '*pero muy interesante!*'

Later, writing my diary, I recalled a stimulating debate at Key West's literary seminar: to what (if any) extent is it permissible for travel writers to embellish or exaggerate incidents – even to enhance narratives with fiction if that makes for a 'better read'? Our divergence of opinion was decisively age-related. The oldies – Peter Matthiessen, Barry Lopez and myself – were adamantly opposed to any element of fiction and only grudgingly tolerant of embellishments and exaggerations. I think it was Barry Lopez who noted that travel writers have a duty of accuracy. By being strictly factual they can make a small but not insignificant contribution to future generations' knowledge of how things were, in countries A, B or C, when they went that way. Someone mentioned Afghanistan as an example. The version of that country's culture and history currently being promoted is counter-balanced or contradicted by such travel writers as Mountstuart Elphinstone, Robert Warburton, George Robertson, Robert Byron, Ella Maillart, Peter Mayne, Eric Newby, Peter Levi (and myself). Incidentally, Peter Levi's perception seems even more painfully keen now than it was when he wrote in 1971: 'As a political entity Afghanistan is nothing but a chewed bone left over on the plate between Imperial Russia and British India.'

All of which leads up to a solemn declaration. I can assure my readers that the foregoing pages give a true and faithful account of the condition of Cuba's Havana-Bayamo rail service in the year AD2006.

Dervla Murphy, now in her eighties, continues to travel the world and is passionate about politics, conservation, bicycling and beer. Her first book, *Full Tilt: Ireland to India with a Bicycle*, was published in 1965 and she has won worldwide praise for over twenty books since.

The above extract is reprinted from *The Island That Dared: Journeys in Cuba*, by kind permission of Eland Publishing (61 Exmouth Market, London EC1R 4QL). © Dervla Murphy 2008

Changing the World's Oldest Profession

Arnold Shirek Chamove

I saw her immediately as I disembarked from the cruise ship: an attractive lady of around thirty watching the mostly over-sixties arrive on Saint Petersburg's quay, most of them looking for coaches to take them to the prescribed sights of the city. She stood quietly, with a self-confidence based on her attractiveness as well as being in her home territory and knowing the ropes. I guessed she was waiting for a single male to approach her. A single male in those lines of passengers snaking out of the cruise terminal was unlikely. The few males were under tight control of their partners.

I usually travel alone, and never take tours but just wander around a new town to get a feel of the place. I poke up narrow alleys to view stuff that is not on show; assess front-garden plants to guess the yearly weather variability and the personality of the inhabitants; wander supermarket aisles to see what's the same and what's different; snack at McDonald's to predict the future of a country's youth and what of the local fashion might be coming to my country.

I want to know the spread of a place – the best and the worst and the normal – like a citizen of the city. But that is impossible for a brief visitor. Who would know Saint Petersburg intimately – who is friendly, will do as asked, and is not weighed down by the teachings of a tourist board?

With those things in mind, I walked up to the lady, remembering the Russian custom of not smiling.

'How much do you charge and for how long?'

With the barest suggestion of friendliness in her face, she quoted fifty US dollars for up to two hours. I later discovered that she was an English teacher in a local comprehensive school at basic secondary level. So I instructed Anya on what I wanted for the fifty bucks and in less than two hours.

I want to see three things in the city, travelling by taxi, I told her, and would like to ask questions as we go. I would like to travel through the poorest part of Saint Petersburg and see the homes there. I would like to travel through the richest residential part of the city. Lastly, with your permission, I would like to see where you live, the food you eat, the ingredients you choose and cooking utensils you use and the books you read.

Cocking her head to one side, she asked, 'Is that very all?'

'Yes, very completely definitely all,' I stated with more confidence than I felt. But off we went, I following like one of her high school students, Anya in charge of taxi negotiations while I listened to the guttural Russian, trying to recognise a word or two, mostly from the numbers that I had memorised on the cruise ship.

Her demeanour softened – a bit. Had I known her long enough to be permitted a smile or would she view me as mentally feeble; or just as a foreigner with different customs?

We saw how the parked cars had no windscreen wipers – taken off so they could not be stolen, Anya explained. We saw how the drain pipes from the buildings emptied onto the footpath (she confirmed that people have to wade through the water when it rains), buildings painted in that ubiquitous pale chartreuse colour, which was popular as it was sold cheaply by the government. Grape vines were used as decoration up the sides of buildings, often just straggling up a scrap of twine or wire. Along the pavement were rows of cherry trees loaded with cherries. 'Yes, edible,' Anya claimed.

It was clearly not a nation of gardeners, judging by what I saw of the city. The common areas in the middle of apartment blocks were not cared for; grass was not cut, trees not pruned nor hedges looked after. No-one planted little patches of colour or even the odd rose bush.

The wealthy areas had fences or concrete walls with rolls of razor wire. In these areas there was no broken concrete on the roadway or pavement, but big old trees. Though not garden aficionados, owners apparently employed men to tend the gardens; they were not gardeners, but the gardens were tidy.

Anya's place looked as if it had been furnished recently in the inexpensive style of the big discount chains. One of her food staples was buckwheat, a grain she used to make a hot oatmeal-like breakfast, pancakes, scones, and other things – *varenyky*, *shashlik* and *borscht*. The walls were covered in photos and bookcases with books in English that I had read as a young adult. We had time for her to tell me the various sides of communism, the good, the bad and the ugly, but from a different viewpoint from what I had learned, one that was more balanced, more believable to a critical academic like myself.

Was my less-travelled choice adventurous? Irresponsible? Something to be frowned upon? It felt a little like that to me, but also rewarding, memorable and innovative. Innovation is looking at something differently, changing its use; taking a problem and turning it into an opportunity and having it work out just fine, thanks. Lucky me. This time thinking outside the box paid off.

Born in San Francisco to a Gold Rush family, **Arnold Shirek Chamove** was educated in the USA and Great Britain. He taught at Stirling University and Massey University and did primate research in Senegal and Gabon. He currently breeds quarter horses and has a business consultancy in New Zealand.

Beyond Google Earth

Marilyn Lacey

Coming from Silicon Valley, I should've known it wouldn't be easy getting to a place not yet mapped by Google Earth.

I chartered the single-engine plane anyway. There it was, squatting like a dusty mosquito on the Lokichokio runway, silhouetted against the one jagged butte that punctuated the otherwise flat expanse. The pilot was inspecting the plane from all angles. He seemed to have no feet; or rather, they appeared to have melted into the shimmering waves of heat that rose from the buckled tarmac. I wondered: could body parts actually melt? And if not, why not? Human life felt fragile in the noon glare of this harsh landscape.

I watched from the shade of an acacia tree as he kicked the tyres and ticked off the inventory. Polio vaccines in the icebox above the jerry can of fuel on the back seat? Check. Boxes of sterile gauze and meds and syringes? Check. Crate of restless chickens pecking beneath the pilot's seat? Check. Carton of lukewarm beer in the hold beneath? Check. Extra water, torch and emergency rations in the backpack? Check. We were good to go. He signalled thumbs up. I grabbed my hat and duffel, left behind sixty-three years of living safely and clambered up over the wing and into the unknown.

For several hours we flew over vast swathes of green and brown: deserts, mountains, grasslands, rivers, swamps. Here and there were clearings where mud-and-thatch huts huddled. Occasionally, a distant dust-swarm raised by the plodding of cattle hooves swirled into the impassive sky. Nothing else. No roads. No development. The noise of our engine was the only intrusion.

That noise alerted the tribes to our coming. The pilot circled Kuron Valley several times, first swooping low to scatter the wildlife away from the dirt track that would serve as our landing strip, then skimming once more a few feet above the dirt to scan for the least uneven, most rock-free path, finally dropping swiftly onto the valley floor and skidding to a stop just yards from a throng of spear-wielding, wildly singing, beautifully tattooed, goatskin-skirted, bare-breasted Toposa women.

We had arrived.

The men, we were told, had gone out to raid cattle from the neighbouring Murle tribe, but these women had streamed down from the surrounding hills to welcome us, singing, clapping, jumping, ululating, dancing and laughing as they helped unload our supplies. The arrival of visitors apparently constituted a major life event.

The Toposa, who do not believe in bathing (ever), pressed around us. Their musty, earthy smell closed in. Everyone wanted to shake hands and touch: skin that had no colour, so unnatural; hair that had no stiffness, so strange. Smiling. Curious. Unafraid. The touchdown of a plane always meant fresh supplies for the clinic that had saved many of them from death by difficult childbirths, crocodile mauling, bouts of malaria, gunshots, snakebite, guinea worm, painful tumours and numberless unnamed ills. We were, therefore, accorded a hero's welcome.

Within moments, however, the hammering heat had wobbled my knees. My vision blurred. The horizon tilted. Was I collapsing?

Melting? The jubilant singing suddenly sounded very far away. Next thing I knew, a nurse had appeared to shepherd me into a pick-up truck for the ride to the clinic, where I flopped onto a cot in a surprisingly dark and cool *tukul*. At that moment I didn't care about the dirt floor, the gaping holes in the mosquito net, the disturbingly large spiders on the mud wall, or the fact that the less-than-clean and visibly rusty cup being offered to me had just been filled with water tapped from an animal bladder suspended from a hook on the ceiling. It was a sheer gift compared to standing unprotected in the equatorial sun. I soon revived.

I was on a mission: document with stories and photos the work being done by the nurses and volunteers whom our non-profit organisation was supporting in this faraway corner of South Sudan, a country just emerging from decades of civil war.

Over the ensuing days I greeted patients in the ward. I remember the gunshot victim whose leg was propped on a box 'for elevation' and whose torso sported raised-bump tattoos that looked like hieroglyphics – stylised birds and plants and streams; the mother sweating and shivering with malaria; the young girl, a suspected survivor of rape, sitting alone in a corner, still too traumatised to talk; the toddler with an abdominal tumour the size of his head. On several afternoons I trekked with the nurses to outlying villages as they vaccinated children. I never really felt at ease seeing the men and boys swaggering with their AK-47s: too reminiscent of the Wild West without a sheriff. (The clinic staff accepted bullets as payment for services; ammunition was more plentiful there than food or firewood.) At the end of the week I was given a wiry Toposa goat for our going-away feast and tried to make it happy during the few hours remaining until its rendezvous with a sharp-edged *panga* in the hands of the cook.

Today the photos hang on my office wall, proof that I made it there and back. Google has since put Kuron on the map, but not before it found its place in my heart. For this I entered the convent forty years ago. For this I am a Sister of Mercy.

Marilyn Lacey, a Sister of Mercy, is Executive Director of Mercy Beyond Borders (www.mercybeyondborders. org, mlacey@mercybeyondborders. org), working with displaced women in South Sudan and Haiti. She holds an MSW from UC Berkeley, three honorary doctorates, and was  personally honoured by the Dalai Lama for her compassion. Her memoir, *This Flowing Toward Me*, was published in 2009.

A Farm in the Cévennes

Janet Rogers

I am alone in the farmhouse. I know I am alone. The farmer left an hour ago. I peered from my bedroom window and saw his white van disappear along the drive, past the linden trees, over the stream and round the corner into the forest.

When I walk down to the kitchen the dog is fast asleep on the mat in front of the fire. The cats are still out hunting. It is 7 a.m. I make coffee and sit at the long wooden table. The dog stirs and moves over to lean against my leg. Maybe he, too, is feeling the isolation. The clock ticks, denting the silence.

I open the door onto the terrace and, coffee cup in hand, walk outside. There is a promising crimson glow behind the mountains. The silhouettes of trees decorate the horizon like black lace. In the valley a grey shadow of mist is floating. Everything is dripping as if someone is trying to fold tissue paper quietly. I hear the sound of sheep's bells.

This is the Cévennes, a remote area of southern France, some thirty-five miles west of Nîmes. I am here for two weeks to improve my French and help with the garden. It's what students do. I am sixty-seven.

It turns out that it's just me and the farmer, Bernard. Bernard's wife left to take a 'cure' two days ago and will return after I have left. And he will be out working much of the time. But she is here in spirit. Her messages are all around – on the front door knocker, on the fridge, on the kitchen cupboards. 'Who am I today and what grand and glorious adventure will I have?' Another says: 'How does it get better than this?' So why did she go?

I should have recognised the warning signs when she phoned, a week before my departure, to say she would not be here. 'But that's fine. Come anyway,' she said. She was cheery and chatty. Then she added: 'By the way, Bernard's not like me. He's fairly quiet.'

Fairly quiet! When my taxi dropped me at the top of the drive yesterday, I looked down on the farmhouse perched on a terrace, pale yellow and stately with dark green shutters. A man was working in the garden, but as I got out of the car and walked down the drive towards the tall trees and garden swing, he disappeared inside.

I assumed it was Bernard, the farmer, my host, but why would he go inside when I approached? He was expecting me. I reached the front door and knocked. I knocked again. The man appeared from a door at the side of the house and introduced himself. It was indeed Bernard. He shook my hand without making eye contact. His head was lowered, his eyes hid behind his heavy rimmed spectacles.

'I'll show you to your room and then I must leave for work,' he said, in French. 'I'll be back late, after nine o'clock. Perhaps you could make some soup for supper.'

I followed Bernard through the corridors of the house and up a staircase to the front section, separated from his living area by two doors. My room was calm and clean, cream tiles on the floor and cream covers on the bed, an old wooden chest and a tiny wrought iron table and chair. I unpacked. I heard a car door slam and realised that Bernard had left for work already.

I looked from my window. On a dull day in October darkness sets in early. The mountains were empty and silent. I saw the smudged shapes of the chestnut trees as they clung to the black slopes. I wondered if I should make my escape and leave before Bernard came back. How would I survive in this lonely, desolate place? But I had no means of escape, no car, no mobile phone reception, no courage to walk in the dark in a land I did not know.

So I went downstairs and chopped vegetables and stroked the cat and patted the dog and prepared soup. And when Bernard returned we ate together, making polite conversation, stilted and difficult.

He gave me instructions as to my tasks, so this morning I am sweeping leaves and cutting lavender. I like cutting lavender. It is like cutting hair, snipping and shaping with scissors, the aroma intense and quite relaxing.

Bernard returns late morning and cooks lunch, a soufflé of spinach and cheese and an endive salad.

The promise of good weather does not materialise. Squalls of rain chase in from the south. Great black clouds shroud the hills. Late in the afternoon it clears a little and I take the dog for a walk. We meander through woods along terraces which drop away steeply down ravines to clear streams. The paths are covered in hundreds of spiky shells, like tiny curled hedgehogs, mouths open, spilling the shiny brown nuts. This is the land of the sweet chestnut, the 'bread tree' as it is known locally.

The sweet chestnut groves cling to the slopes as the people here have clung to life in the past. In times of famine it is the sweet chestnut which has sustained them.

Later Bernard calls me into the kitchen. He is making chestnut jam. 'I thought you might like to watch.'

This is no ordinary jam, no sticky, sweet-smelling fruit, just a bowl of what looks like semolina. Bernard adds sugar syrup to the large bowl of floury mixture and stirs it with a wooden spoon.

'It looks a bit like wallpaper paste,' I venture. He turns and for the first time since my arrival, he smiles. I watch and he continues to stir and as the steam rises in the farmhouse kitchen, a pleasant aroma emerges of rum and vanilla mixed with a sweet nuttiness.

He stirs until the mixture becomes gloopy and great pits appear, like the surface of the moon. Gradually it changes to a dark honey colour and the jam is ready for potting. After supper, Bernard stirs a large spoonful into a bowl of natural yoghurt and we have a delicious dessert.

I am beginning to relax, to content myself with French thoughts and just a few French words; to settle into life in this place where I can walk all afternoon without seeing another soul, no sound of traffic, just the crack of a twig breaking beneath my boot and the trickling of water in the streams, and where I can find a different rhythm of life.

I think we will get along, me and this quiet man who, I fear, I will never really know.

Janet Rogers worked as a news reporter in her twenties and returned to writing when she retired. She has won several national travel writing competitions and her articles have appeared in the UK and Australian press. She lives by the sea in West Sussex and is a keen cyclist and skier.

Roads to Savannakhet

Susan Ross

A t last, here was my transport. I had waited three hours by a *cà phê*, or coffee, stall on a corner of littered wasteland. Now this vehicle, roof loaded to double its height, tyres bulging almost flat to the dusty road, had pulled to a shuddering halt in front of me. So many buses in so many countries over the years, but none quite like this one. I was the final passenger to board before the long journey over the border to Savannakhet.

I hoisted my small weather-beaten rucksack, preparing to enter. Huge, bulky jute sacks labelled 'Sugar' and 'Fertiliser', piled high, blocked my way. Was this a 'luxury' bus or an incendiary device? And how should I advance? Encouraging hands drew me inwards and upwards.

'*Falang, falang*, bring in.' I crested the cargo, emerging into a narrow airspace beneath the faded pink velveteen ceiling, near to the blackened and unusable air conditioning vents. The whole body of the vehicle was filled, top to bottom, front to back, with the misshapen sacks. If there was an aisle, it lay buried deep beneath. The human cargo reclined, without choice in this matter, in various positions tight against each other.

I felt a moment of claustrophobia.

'Put the falang front.' I crawled forward on my belly next to a lady who, supine, drew up her bony knees to allow me into a small niche adjacent to the windows, of which maybe twenty centimetres showed above the undulating cargo, allowing air and a view. Falang, or foreigners, like to look; after all, that's one of the reasons we are here.

The vehicle was already moving heavily forward, the gear lever grating against the worn metal floor. I removed my boots, and located my scrappy card of useful vocabulary, already heavily creased. As always, the passengers were happy to engage.

'Nine hours?'

'*Không*,' came the reply, 'No. Bus very slow to Lao Báo.'

Newspaper wrappings and seed shells spread around us. The day wore on, people slept, and I reclined, content as always to be moving across the country in this way, with these people.

Then, a momentary release from our transport for the short walk between the two border posts, and onwards towards Xépôn.

I knew of this town, situated near the old Ho Chi Minh Trail. Maybe twenty years ago I had travelled a different road to Savannakhet, one from Vientiane in the north. A road was being built, a journey of fifteen hours of red dust. A smaller vehicle, even less comfort, no sacks to cushion the unyielding metal seats that threw me forward over every undulation. I'd had company for that journey: an Australian I had met who had returned to Laos to look for a place that had been important to him many years earlier. In the war, shot down from his helicopter, he had been the only survivor. His return to Xépôn was to enlist the help of a villager, and then send a pig ahead on a leash to search for the place. In Savannakhet, I received the news, 'Difficult to be sure, everything has changed.' And Savannakhet had been poor and dusty, with the small-town sweetness of its Buddhist people. Now I gazed out at the wood and bamboo houses of Xépôn, and some of concrete, and wondered if the town had changed much. The bus began to gather some speed on downhill stretches. This was a 'good' road, people said, but of course it was not. Darkness fell, with its familiar Lao velvety warmth.

I had left Vietnam when it became cold in the north, the watery rice fields brown and grey, the trains and buses clammy with condensation. In Son Trach with its spellbindingly beautiful caves, I had become uncomfortable in the chill, despite my guest house having clean sheets and hot tap water. Accordingly, I had devised a plan to heat my damp bed. I placed cans of soft drinks and my water bottle in the steaming washbasin. Cautiously I then put them into my bed, wrapping damp clothes around another outside the bed. This was so good; I slept peacefully in a dry warm bed, surrounded by cans and bottles. I carefully repeated the manoeuvre the following day and, moving a can into the bed, was almost thrown backwards as a spray of brown liquid burst into the air. The deluge covered sheets, pillows, duvet, ceiling, and myself. Horrified, I attempted to clean it all; my excuses to the owner involved numerous apologies, a lie concerning a faulty ring-pull, and some small remuneration.

But now I was continuing west, the bus passing small dark villages, a few lamps or candles bringing patches of soft yellow light to the blackness. Banana leaves flapped against the sides of the bus. Families were squatting on makeshift wooden verandas, dipping into bowls of rice, calling playing children away from our wheels. Women were washing plates next to huge terracotta urns, ubiquitous throughout Laos. Later I caught a glimpse of a boy, maybe nine or ten years old, sitting on an old wooden chair outside his darkened home, writing in his school books beneath the single dim street lamp.

At about ten o'clock the bus slowed, the noise of the heavy metal gears waking some of the sleeping passengers. Then we stopped. We were in what appeared to be a large village of mainly unlit wooden houses, but a few market stalls had lamplight.

'Now, now, you off, here,' someone said. The woman next to me pressed my hand and smiled.

'*Laa kawn,*' I responded. 'Goodbye.' I pulled my boots on and grasped my rucksack, sliding on my back towards the doorway, dropping clumsily far down into the bottom of the stairwell, and onto the road. Two other passengers, falang too, who had been lying in the back of the bus, climbed down and stood next to me, uncertainly trying to focus in the semi-darkness.

This surely wasn't Savannakhet, maybe just a bus halt on the outskirts of town. I looked at a middle-aged man who was sitting at the front of one of the stalls, chewing a type of tobacco. '*Sabaidee*, Savannakhet?' I asked twice, with a question in my voice.

'No,' he replied. A cloud of diesel fumes enveloped us as the bus made its departure, lumbering onwards into the night, maybe all the way north to Vientiane. Its one small tail light, the left one, receded into the dust and the dark. 'Savannakhet... *kai thao dai?*' I tried again. The man held up three fingers. I looked at the other weary travellers. 'Do you think that means three or thirty?'

Another man moved forward. '*Songthaew*... taxi? Fifty thousand kip. *Saam sip* kilometres.' Another thirty kilometres! The bus driver had left us near the north-south route that I had travelled many years before. Price negotiations followed, and at last the three of us climbed into the back of an old van. It was littered with droppings and corn stalks and leaves, but at least we were upright. We continued slowly, the van veering across the road when its feeble headlights illuminated a particularly large hole, or an unilluminated cyclist.

At last we saw more lights ahead. My fellow travellers were bound for the centre of town, but I had a more exotic destination. No wandering the streets tonight searching for budget accommodation. With a little foresight concerning the probable length of this journey I had made previous online arrangements for a comfortable bed. Our morose driver smiled broadly when I mentioned my hotel; he appeared to know it well. We continued along the potholed streets until we suddenly came out of the darkness into light. A lot of light. I looked out in amazement as we turned into a long avenue with lawns, clipped trees, ornate electric lamps and elephants: numerous larger than life grey elephants made of resin. This apparent hallucination continued as we approached an enormous building and came to a clattering halt under a wide canopy flanked by yet more elephants. A stretch limousine was parked to one side. A liveried doorman reached for my dusty rucksack.

'Goodbye, good luck,' I called to my companions, who gaped in amazement. I entered the palatial lobby and arrived at a long marble reception desk staffed by three immaculate Lao girls and an equally immaculate young man who spoke some English. Formalities completed, I was led to a glass lift which ascended an interior wall to the second floor. Beneath my astonished gaze spread a cavernous space, gaudily decorated, with gaming tables and a handful of players. The lift whirred to a halt, the glass doors slid back, and I was escorted along a fashionably carpeted corridor towards my room. When I turned to look back, a thin trail of broken corn leaves and stalks indicated the route I had taken.

Susan Ross's mother said to her when she was forty-seven, 'Time goes so quickly, Susie, you have to get on with life.' So she did. She had always loved travelling independently, and was lucky to be able to continue this with even longer and harder journeys all around the world.

The Kindness of Strangers

Nick Gibbons

Careering along the 1,795-metre Tukh Manuk Pass in southern Armenia, I clutched the steering wheel of the small delivery vehicle while the driver operated the van's pedals and took photographs of us, and wondered what on earth our friends and family back home would think if they could see us.

My wife Jean and I have always been keen travellers but it wasn't until I turned fifty in 2000 that I began cycle touring with a group of friends known as the 'Topsham Old Gits'. Over the years that followed I persuaded Jean to get on her bike as well. We have since discovered the pleasure of travelling through countries at a sedate pace. In this way we are forced to break our journeys in out-of-the-way places where the locals often see few visitors.

Tours through Europe were followed by more exotic destinations such as Jordan, Syria and Laos, with a great sense of achievement at successfully completing long rides of a scale that we probably couldn't have imagined in our youth. When we announce our latest plans, our acquaintances tend to ask two questions: 'Are you going in a group?' and 'Isn't it dangerous?' The answer to both questions is a resolute 'No'.

In 2012 we set off on a two-week tour taking in parts of Georgia and Armenia. Given our advancing years, we aren't proud and don't insist on pedalling every single kilometre. On this trip our cycling was to start at the monastery of Khor Virap near the foot of Mount Ararat, and since we only had a limited time, we had ordered a large taxi to take us and the bikes the thirty kilometres from our hotel in the suburbs of Yerevan, the Armenian capital, to our starting point. After a visit to the monastery, we were to cycle seventy kilometres over the Tukh Manuk pass to Areni in the Armenian wine-growing region.

It is always important for cyclists to have a hearty breakfast to set them up for the day's exercise. That day, besides bread, jam, salad and scrambled eggs, it also included sausage and mashed potatoes. Well fuelled, we checked out of the hotel and waited to be collected. Promptly at 9 a.m. a taxi rolled up; it was a beautifully polished, gleaming new vehicle but could not by any stretch of the imagination be described as large. There was no way that we, our bikes and panniers were going to be squeezed into it.

Negotiations with the hotel receptionist and the taxi driver were to no avail and so, just after 9.30 a.m., there was nothing for it but to cycle out of the city and hope to make up lost time during the day.

Navigating a major city on a bike is often a tricky undertaking and doing this in Yerevan was no exception. I used my rudimentary Russian to ask a taxi driver for directions. He probably noticed my slightly furrowed brow at his lengthy response and so suggested leading us out of the city for a very small fee. This was an excellent idea, not least due to the almost total lack of signposts. We formed a convoy – the taxi, its three functioning emergency lights flashing, followed by me with Jean bringing up the rear, her legs a blur of motion as she tried to keep up the pace. Soon we were safely on the hard shoulder of the dual carriageway leading towards the Iranian border. We had a tailwind and speeded along with hills to our left and the militarised Turkish border with its lookout posts to our right; because of past conflicts, Armenia has open borders with only two of its four neighbouring countries.

Khor Virap is a place of pilgrimage due to its connection with Saint Gregory the Illuminator and has a magnificent view of Mount Ararat – so the guidebooks say – but on that October day the weather was rather hazy and the summit was obscured. We had to content ourselves with a look around the two churches, one of which included a nerve-wracking sixty-metre descent via a steep metal ladder into the stuffy cell where Saint Gregory had been imprisoned for twelve years – definitely not advisable for claustrophobics. After that we were very glad to re-emerge blinking into the daylight in order to carry on with our ride.

We mounted our bikes and pedalled off, wondering whether we would reach our destination by nightfall, but then disaster struck: a link in Jean's chain had become slightly twisted and detached. Our hearts sank. I have only done a two-hour cycle maintenance course and changing an inner tube is about the limit of my ability. I possess a chain-breaker but as I don't know how to use one, it really is more for decorative purposes. What were we to do? Was our eight-hundred-kilometre tour going to be ruined on the first day?

We limped into the small, nearby village of Pokr Vedi, which, unsurprisingly, had no cycle repair shop. That's when we had a stroke of luck in the form of Martin, a gentleman of about our age, who came along on a bike that was also about our age. There are very few cyclists in Armenia so he was a rare and welcome sight. I managed to flag him down and show him the problem. Martin nodded wisely, got back on his bike, cycled a little way down the road and knocked on an old door. It creaked open and another elderly gentleman emerged. This, as we later discovered, was Karl.

After studying the chain from various angles, Karl went back inside and returned with an ancient toolbox. Martin, Karl and his brother banged and hammered on the chain for about half an hour and finally managed to fix it, thus saving the day. By this time everyone's hands were filthy and covered with oil, so Karl invited us into his tiny home to clean our hands with some remarkably effective washing powder. This was the point when we were introduced to the famed Armenian hospitality. It was time for lunch and Karl and his brother produced for us fresh *lavash*, the delicious Armenian flatbread, as well as cheese, tomatoes, peppers and coffee. Karl even popped out into his garden and cut us a couple of huge bunches of grapes. Making conversation in a mixture of extremely broken Russian and English while sampling the wonderful food, we rapidly learnt the Russian word *vkusni*, which means 'scrumptious'. Sadly, time was passing all too quickly and soon, with grapes securely strapped to our panniers, it was time for us to bid farewell to our helpers, who refused any payment for their hard work.

By now we knew there was no way we would have time to cycle over a mountain pass and reach our destination under our own steam. Nevertheless, as a lifelong supporter of Exeter City, a lower division English football team, I am an optimist so we carried on regardless. Irritatingly, the wind direction had changed and was no longer helping. On the positive side, the clouds did lift and majestic, snow-capped Mount Ararat became visible. We reached the small, dusty town of Yeraskh just before 4 p.m.

Yeraskh has a café and a few shops but most importantly a roundabout where all the traffic has to slow down and take a left turn, as the road straight ahead leads to the closed border between Armenia and Azerbaijan. Realising that two oldies like us were not going to be able to conquer the pass by sundown, we threw in the towel, positioned ourselves just beyond the roundabout and started hitchhiking. There wasn't much traffic but after about fifteen minutes a driver in a small delivery van stopped and loaded us into the front and our bikes into the back. This was the very friendly Noash, who was taking supplies back to his grocery shop in the provincial capital of Yeghegnadzor. He seemed so delighted to have our company that as we rattled along, he took out his mobile phone and called his wife to let her know that he had a couple of aged, foreign hitchhikers on board.

As the road wound its way up to the pass, we admired the mountains and deep ravines. Jean was busy taking photos of the scenery. Incredibly, it was at this point that Noash started urging me to take the wheel. This seemed a touch risky but he was very insistent. Since I have experience of driving in Switzerland, I have often taken a car over mountain passes so I accepted. Then Noash decided he should borrow Jean's camera to take photos of us while still operating the pedals. It was a white-knuckle ride.

Although Noash invited us to travel on with him, meet his family and stay the night with them, at the top of the pass we regretfully said goodbye. We wanted to enjoy the nineteen-kilometre whizz down to the valley floor and we needed to spend the night in Areni in order to visit the impressive tenth-century Noravank Monastery first thing the next day. As we descended at breakneck speed, we knew we were approaching our destination by the roadside stands where people sold homemade wine in Coca-Cola bottles. Only later did I discover that this was not a form of recycling, but a way of camouflaging the wine for Iranian truck drivers who wanted to take alcohol back home.

As dusk fell, we arrived at the gorge and found, to our delight, a brand-new hotel which also offered evening meals. Enjoying huge bowls of *borscht* and sampling the local wine, we decided that it had been a day like no other. Would the famously hospitable Armenians have been so helpful towards a younger, fitter couple or did they feel particularly sorry for two oldies in distress – who is to say? All I know is that the kindness of strangers that day has left an indelible mark on both of us.

Nick Gibbons is sixty-four and grew up in Devon. After a two-year spell working in a bank, he returned to fulltime education. He has been teaching English in Switzerland since 1973. He and his wife Jean took up cycling relatively late in life and spend most of their holidays exploring foreign countries.

Last Days in Kadugli

Ruth Keene

'I sleep beside you tonight,' murmured Ibrahim, looking up from stirring the coffee he was brewing over the gas ring.

'Tempting,' I thought, basking in the protective strength emanating from this husky hero of derring-do. He was rigged out daily in differing shades of camouflage, topped by his wine-red beret with its badge, a pair of shiny brass gold wings. 'Airborne,' he stated proudly. 'I protect you from the guards.'

We were in a whitewashed old farmhouse in a busy, dusty side street in Kadugli in the Nuba Mountains in the geographical centre of Sudan. It was mostly open to the air, so welcome breezes cooled the house. We usually sat in the 'salon', a kind of lean-to fronted with mesh stretched between tree branches. Badr, our landlord, had reassured us the night before, 'No mosquitoes here, look, we have wire,' conveniently ignoring the gaping hole between the screen and the partly-demolished wall. Dust was everywhere, that special red Sudanese choking dust, stinging my puffy eyes, grating my rasping throat, in my nose and covering my clothes.

Ibrahim had just returned after another mysterious disappearance. Waiting for him to return, we had spent the evening talking to Badr, making difficult conversation in poor Arabic on my side and poor English on his. He was an elegant Sudanese man of mixed blood from Port Sudan, his Arab origins obvious in his sinuous walk and tall, graceful frame. In Port Sudan, he told us, he had many businesses, a big house with air conditioning, not like here.

Badr was due to move into this house in ten days with his bride-to-be, a beautiful young girl with light skin and Arab features – he showed us her photograph on his phone – and Ibrahim had somehow persuaded him to let us spend two nights here. The new furniture, imported with difficulty from Khartoum, stood in its plastic coverings around the courtyard, incongruous in this rustic building: a massive, green-veneered wardrobe, plump sunshine-yellow armchairs and matching settees, looking somehow forlorn, waiting to be claimed.

'Paah,' suddenly spat out Olga, my colleague and current travelling companion, grinding yet another cigarette stub into the ground with fury. 'He go, he come back maybe tomorrow, I tell you, he no good, take money, go… Zees iz not real militerry.'

My retirement project to perfect my Arabic by travelling through Sudan teaching English was not working out quite as I might have hoped. Olga was not easily coming to terms with the differences between Macedonian and Sudanese culture.

'I get invoice from your shop, Badr,' Ibrahim had said, 'be back five minutes.' Experience had told us this would be around five hours at a conservative estimate, and we were unfortunately being proved right. It was after three of those hours had passed that we realised Ibrahim had given only part of our rent payment to Badr and taken the rest with him.

'He use money,' gloomily predicted Badr. 'Should show more respect for grey hair.'

The house was divided by a rough-hewn wall to mark male and female quarters, and in the adjoining courtyard we could hear the steady murmur of the four young soldiers assigned to guard us should anyone show undue interest in our possessions or even view us as potentially lucrative hostages. From time to time we would glimpse them on our way to the aromatic corner Ibrahim had indicated as our modern toilet. The lack of running water, and overuse by so many temporary residents, had provided fertile ground for the white burrowing insects which emerged from the putrid hole, usually as I needed to squat over it.

The young guards, raw recruits I guessed, seemed unfamiliar with the menacing AK-47s they carried carelessly, or rested against their stools. I did not find the constant clank of metal against metal reassuring.

Finally, as I was starting to think about snuggling down in my silk sleeping bag, wondering if I could last until the morning without another visit to that awful toilet, there was a loud knocking at the gate, and Ibrahim returned. Fortunately for him and for my burgeoning skills as a mediator, Olga was already fast asleep. I had been sitting in the courtyard, mesmerised by the sight of so many stars, brilliant in this desolate desert setting. His offer of coffee as we sat together enjoying the stellar show was very welcome, and cleverly took the sting out of any comments I might have made.

He was tall, imposing in all his guises: as a paratrooper in rust-coloured camouflage, as a ranger in dust-coloured camouflage, as ethnic Sudanese in flowing white *galabeya* and white skullcap or more conventionally in faded jeans and pink striped shirt – in all of these his muscular frame and shining black skin radiated strength.

After some companionable chatting, we both retired – separately – for the night, thinking about the next day, the last day. That was when we learned the unexplained reason for Ibrahim's absence and the discrepancy in the rent.

He had needed the money to pay the carpenter who had made our farewell presents.

Born in post-war Wales, **Ruth Keene** reared a family after university and worked in post-independence Zambia; then spent twenty years in multilingual Luxembourg, tending to the family while developing European languages working in a bank and European Institutions.  Post-marriage, she taught English in the Middle East and Sudan to learn Arabic (and is still learning).

Time to Enjoy the Moment

Wish You Were Here

Kay Wiseman

People have been stopping me in corridors and asking in hushed tones, 'What will you do now?' I leave the office for the last time with a clutch of cheeky 'Happy Retirement' cards and a grin on my face. I know exactly what I am going to do now.

A week later I see the Blue Mosque, the pomegranate sellers and the grey Bosphorus from under an umbrella. The heavens open over Istanbul. Drenching rain and wind do not let up. Sagging awnings and dripping, battered bamboo overhangs offer some shelter in the Old City as I wander past glittering shops with dimly lit interiors and bored shopkeepers.

I find a small eating house where the waiters do not blink at a single woman of a certain age coming in from the rain to eat alone. The cooking of Istanbul inherits many elements of Ottoman court cuisine with a lighter use of spices and a wider availability of vegetable stews. Every dish delights my taste buds. I go back each evening and by the third night, an American couple are shooed off my usual table when I appear. The waiters flirt and flit around me like hummingbirds; I meet all the behind-the-scenes staff and I feel they would probably take me home if I stayed any longer.

This is not tourist season and I soon notice that when I do meet other travellers, especially those from England, they look over my shoulder expectantly. Finding no husband lurking in the shadows, their reaction is always the same. 'Travelling alone? Oh, I could never do that.' The Turks ask, 'But *where is* your husband?'

I create an imaginary husband. Over the next few days, the excuses for his absence become more and more outlandish.

Seeking refuge from the rain, I come upon a hammam. With visions of steamy rooms and relaxing hours in a cocoon of warmth, scents and music under domed ceilings with cut-out stars, Turkish baths of dreams, I make my way in. Not being able to speak nor read the signs I happily step over the threshold, hold out some coins to a man in a ticket box with a grille and turn to find myself face to face with a lady sumo wrestler.

With no hint of delicacy she strips me of my clothes and pushes me into a sauna. There is no towel with which to pretend modesty. A beautiful, young naked girl arrives and lies down to sizzle.

I'm not very good in saunas, so I decide to go in search of the more soothing part of my imaginary experience. I exit only to be accosted by the big lady once more who seems flustered by my early appearance. She physically nudges me into another room where I am alone again.

This room is circular, all marble and quite cold. It has a high barrel ceiling and vibrant decorative tiles surrounding small basins with overhanging brass taps set into the walls. In the centre is what looks like a sacrificial altar and I am clearly the one to be sacrificed.

The young girl from the sauna now enters with the large lady and without ceremony they begin to douse me, alternating bowls of warm and cold water and laughing at my feeble squeaks. Together they have me cornered and bustle me onto the marble plinth.

I am being British and trying to take all of this in my stride. But at the next move, I close my eyes in disbelief.

The young girl now straddles me, stark naked, and begins to soap me down vigorously with a rather rustic loofa which seems to be made of barbed wire. With all this soap and water and marble I begin to slip and slide worryingly towards the edge of the marble slab, which elicits raucous laughter from my two 'therapists'. The sumo wrestler sets to kneading me to a pulp and only gives up when I feel like tenderised steak. More sloshing and pummelling follows and finally, weak, bedraggled, dazed and beaten, my dreams of warm, scented and relaxing Turkish baths shattered, I am handed a towel and allowed to make my escape.

Having seen much of this dripping city with Europe behind and Asia in front, I fly to Kayseri and the promise of a cave hotel in Cappadocia. My room is carved into the hills, beautifully furnished with rich fabrics of intricate design, colours of hot earth and deep exotic nights. I step out onto a terrace which offers a free cabaret of unpolluted night skies. Time stands still on these starlit nights and I time-travel back to an era where caravans crossed vast plains en route to trade in Damascus and beyond.

Cappadocia is full of otherworldly natural sites. Coming from a childhood in South Africa I first liken the tall, cone-shaped rock formations to giant ant hills. The countryside is semi-arid and the 'fairy chimneys' are the end product of thousands of years of geological sculpting. On the surface all looks tranquil and timeless but archaeologists have recently uncovered a massive underground city, descending eleven levels and stretching several miles. They have found tunnels, hidden churches, stables, tombs and escape galleries with artefacts dating back five thousand years. They calculate around twenty thousand people lived here, underground.

There is a continental collision near the city of Van, 605 miles to the west, whilst I am here, but on this wide open plain in the clusters of hamlets, daily life rolls on, undisturbed as it has been for centuries. Ragged children with beaming faces stare as I walk by. Pointing and giggling, they follow until they get bored or their mothers hiss at them to stop teasing the tourist. The men sitting outside cafés playing cards ignore me completely with not the slightest hint of curiosity.

I am told by my waiter at the hotel that in the early hours of each morning, when the horizon gropes for tinges of colour, there are people blowing up balloons, great big balloons.

Arriving by jeep in the dark I am dropped off in the middle of a field where I can just make out the shape of a sleepy, partially inflated hot air balloon on its side. I am offered a pre-flight breakfast by candlelight and eerily, out of the gloom, clutches of people of different nationalities begin to appear. Tour companies have discovered Cappadocia. It all makes for a surreal scene.

As a lone traveller I am invited to clamber into a basket full of Korean ladies. With much bowing and smiling and giggling and paying not a jot of attention to the pilot's emergency landing instructions, we gently drift up to meet the pink and tangerine fingers of sunrise.

As we lazily gain height, my basket-mates quieten down and stop pointing iPads at each other, tamed by the dreaminess of the flight. The light increases and we are suddenly aware of other balloons colourfully dancing in the air both above and below. We are in a Dali painting.

Squeals of alarm come when our pilot deliberately skims the top of an almond tree and then whooshes the burners to take us up high again before all too soon we tumble back to earth. The basket gently bounces and then turns on its side as the balloon floppily succumbs to being tethered in the field.

These are moments I want to hold on to forever. The colours of the balloons floating over the earth, the sense of mystic peace, the smells of early morning and the feeling that time has stopped and all is well in the world.

My basket-mates insist on kissing me goodbye and taking photographs as we sip champagne and toast the pilot, the balloon and the sunrise with more bowing.

I send a card back to the office: Wish you were here!

Kay Wiseman was introduced to travel by a pink Union Castle mail ship bound for South Africa. The pitching Bay of Biscay and sliding soup dishes did not put her off. Prospective employers were always asked 'Will there be any travel involved?' If the answer was 'Yes,' she took the job. Kay has worked in advertising, public relations and the hotel industry. Now retired, she writes reviews for Silver Travel Advisor.

Tugela Gorge

Jean Ashbury

'Nooo. Not true. Mama looks too young,' said the Zulu ranger. He'd clocked I was a senior citizen as I signed the mountain register at the Royal Natal National Park. Seeing his admiration, I preened and thanked my five-a-day regime (and the gods, yoga and Pilates) for holding back the decades, at least from my face.

'Hear that,' I said to Gordon, my partner. He wasn't listening. He was too busy with a map, calculating how long it would take to walk to Tugela Gorge. As he's a veteran mountaineer, I let him get on with it. Making no allowances for arthritic knees and hips functioning on borrowed time, he estimated six hours for the fourteen-kilometre round trip and entered our return time in the mountain register. We'd get back by four, sign out and have a snooze before beers at sunset and a *braai*.

I wanted to sit outside our chalet watching the guinea fowls forage and the light changing on the Drakensberg escarpment, but a second chance to see Tugela Falls was too good to be missed.

Our base was at Thendele, a hutted camp inside the park. Every chalet has its own stupendous view of the Amphitheatre. This five-kilometre-long cliff is the icon for South Africa's dragon mountains, the Drakensbergs, and leaping down it are Tugela Falls, the second-highest in the world. Twenty years before, we'd scrambled through the sandstone 'Tunnel' at the entrance to the gorge and onto a mess of boulders. That was in the dry season. The river was a trickle, the falls non-existent.

The trail from Thendele to the foot of the falls is an easy gradient. It meanders through the veld into a forest of yellowwood trees then drops down to the riverbed. It is well-walked and requires only average fitness, but the last kilometre and a half entails crossing the Tugela River three times.

I stood on the path overlooking the valley. The morning smelt of rain. Bloated from a storm during the night, the river looked like an overfed silver python on the move.

'Looks too high for –'

'Might be okay further upstream.'

The Amphitheatre was streaked with tinsel-like falls that told a different story, as had the stream from Devil's Hoek that rushed under the bridge we'd crossed earlier.

'We don't have to go all the way, do we? I want to walk, not swim.'

I was not to be let off. 'Just a little boulder-hopping at the end to get across to the gorge. Then we'll go up the chain ladder.'

High-altitude trekking, rock climbing, rope ladders, chain ladders, boulder hopping… All had been done not so long ago, but caution had crept up on me. Gone were my gung-ho days of going for it. In came doubts about my body's ability to perform the adventures in my mind. I started to see a kaleidoscope of slipping and falling and fractures.

It was a Sunday morning. Day trippers and determined Nordic walkers wielding poles were out in dozens. The young and fit sped past with 'scuse mes and thank yous as the old and slow got out of their way. I watched their disappearing backs and imagined their lithe bodies leaping from rock to rock without a thought for helicopter rescues.

The trail hauled upwards, enough for my thighs to protest. About two kilometres on, we came to Policeman's Helmet, a rusty-pink sandstone outcrop resembling the pith helmet Michael Caine wore low over his brow in *Zulu*. The film tells the story of the Battle of Rorke's Drift in 1879, and it was shot in and around the Drakensbergs. I ate chocolate raisins, thought about the standoff between the British Army and the Zulu warriors, and said, 'Chain ladder.'

'What?'

'Not doing it.'

Near the mouth of the gorge, the fifty-foot chain ladder dangles down bare rock. It's a baby compared to others in the Drakensbergs. On my previous visit I'd clambered up for fun. The knee-wobbling and heart-fluttering had given me the adrenalin rush I craved, but on this occasion, I had no desire for that.

We pressed on. The river flashed below. The Amphitheatre drew nearer. The yellowwood forest opened to the river bed and we met walkers straggling back. They'd balked at the first river crossing, which was not as bad as I had anticipated. Rocks strewn in the river were reachable without too much of a stretch. Water barely touched the uppers of my boots. Ditto for the second crossing. Then came the third: big, cinnamon-coloured boulders spaced too far for my leprechaun legs.

'Jump,' said Gordon. He had leapt like a mountain goat and was standing precariously on a rock, arms outstretched as if inviting me to waltz. Sweet but daft said my brain. If I missed his hand, I'd be in the river. If he caught me and slipped…

I waded into the knee-deep, screamingly chilly water.

Drying out by a crystal clear rock pool with pebbles smooth as jelly beans, I watched him head for the chain ladder.

'Come on,' he said, but I stayed put.

The river gurgled, the sun and clouds played tag above the Devil's Tooth, a needle of rock. I inhaled the freshness of mountain wilderness and felt free from bucket lists. I will probably never see Tugela Falls, but I will remember walking through swathes of fiery-red bottlebrush flowers, proteas with green leaves translucent in the sun and bright Namaqua daisies; I will remember lammergeyers chasing circles in the sky, and most of all the beauty and silence of the mountains.

Growing older has slowed me down, not killed my sense of adventure but made me rethink what I want to see in the world. It has made me aware that travel is not just about rushing to bag known wonders but also about seeing the small things that create the beauty of places. In the words of Marcel Proust: 'The real voyage of discovery consists not in seeking new landscapes but in having new eyes.'

Jean Ashbury was born in Trinidad in the Caribbean but lives in London. She has been ambling about the world for a while and has a love of mountains and wild places. She was highly commended in the Bradt/*Independent on Sunday* Travel Writing Competition in 2014.

The Road Always Calling

Owen Clough

Itchy feet – that has always been our problem, and ten years ago my wife and I decided to do something about it. I wasn't quite at the retirement age of sixty-five, but it was now or never.

We bought a nine-metre American fifth wheeler; included with the package was a truck, which wasn't new but it would do. Our plan was to travel the length and breadth of our own country, New Zealand, for a few years. In fact, it's been ten years and we're still going.

We rented out our house and took to the road. One thing we learned right away is that American motorhomes are not made for New Zealand roads. Away from the highly populated areas, our roads are winding, steep and narrow. We nevertheless stuck to the secondary roads, visiting places on and off the beaten track. We crossed between the two islands five times and only once had a calm sailing. Eight-metre waves chucked us around like a cork in a bottle, yet this was all part of experiencing our country, even though I was crook as a dog the first three times.

Our truck has never let us down, but our van, or motorhome, has. On a wet and stormy night in Auckland, peak period, as I was travelling down a road on a slight hill at twenty kilometres per hour, I touched the brakes and the next thing I knew, the van had jackknifed around to the side of the truck. The van weighs five tons, and it pushed the truck to the opposite side of the road. Even today I cannot understand how I did not hit another car. Thankfully the angels were on our side, and there was a gap in the traffic. The van took three months to fix and as we were living in it, the repairers had to work around us.

Back on the road, we travelled to the top of the North Island as far as Cape Reinga, following the beaches in the summer, and in the middle of winter sometimes we did a bit of house-sitting in New Zealand or Australia.

Watching the trout rise on a river in the South Island on an autumn morning with the mist clinging to the water and only my wife and I to see it, what a pleasure it was to be alive. Midsummer sunset after 10 p.m. in Southland, the wild west coast of New Zealand where the waves smash the rocky coastline after travelling across the Tasman Sea, and native bush creeps down to the sea, untouched since the days when Captain Cook saw this land on his 1769 voyage of discovery. The blowholes at Punakaiki on a good southwesterly wind send the water a hundred metres high all around us. Glaciers slide down from the Southern Alps into rainforest – the only place in the world where this happens. The population is sparse on the west coast and it is a pleasure to drive – carefully, though, as the road twists and turns up and down, and our rig is very slow so we are always pulling off to let any traffic go past. The top of the South Island is the start of the Heaphy Track: no internet, no phone and, unless you have a satellite dish, no TV, just the bush, sea and the sound of birds. Good fishing in the sea.

Back south, we cross the Southern Alps to Te Waikoropupu Springs (Pupu for short), the largest freshwater springs in the world.

Then over the hill to Totaranui, golden beaches and native bush, where you can walk the Abel Tasman Track in the national park named after the Dutch explorer. Not enough hours in the day to do everything, and every night – with birdsong in the air as the sun slips down behind the hills – we feel alive and at peace.

Following the east coast south through the wine country of Marlborough, we stop at Peter Jackson's Omaka Aviation Heritage Centre, a museum of World War I aircraft. Lunch, dinner, let's stay a week, never in a hurry… then on to whale and dolphin watching at Kaikoura. The evenings sitting outside our van with the Pacific Ocean at our door, we watch a pod of over a hundred dolphins come into the bay to feed with their young. What a privilege to be the only ones to see it.

Back down Highway One is Christchurch, where we are from, our broken city. We are back in town for the 2010 earthquakes. Once we see our place is OK, we drive south to the big rivers that flow from the Alps to the sea, salmon run and the fishing is good and as the days start to draw in we decide it is time to head back to the winterless north.

Crossing over once again on the ferry to the capital, Wellington, with a brief stay to look at the national museum, we cross over the Rimutaka hills, passing small towns, to the east coast and out to the Castle Point lighthouse, then follow the road as it twists and turns north. In a few years' time, as we pass this area again, we will buy a section to use as a base, to hole up for the winter.

Around the East Cape where the crayfish are to die for, then on to the Bay of Plenty, and Mount Maunganui where the surf is good and the beach is fine sand. Moving, always moving, up to the Coromandel coast to dig holes in the sand at the hot water beach

– your own sauna, a great place to stop in the middle of winter and therapeutic as well. Head north, just keep heading north as the days close in, to park at a Department of Conservation camp overlooking a crescent beach with the crashing of waves to send you off to sleep each night and the temperature not dropping below ten degrees throughout the winter.

All the way up in Northland, where both our families come from, we feel at home as we explore the roads of Hokianga: the sand dunes as high as hills, the largest harbour in New Zealand. Then it's back down the west coast as the sun gets stronger, passing Auckland once again and down to the volcano cone of Taranaki. We cross the country on the forgotten highway through the bush and tunnels, seeing very little traffic, passing the volcanic plateau of Tongariro, the three volcanoes all quiet at the moment. We come to the largest lake in the country, Lake Taupo, with pumice on the shore line, good for cleaning pots and taking the unwanted dead skin off your heels, and up to the thermal area of Rotorua with steam, mud pools, geysers and the smell of sulphur strong in the air.

At Christmas we catch up with our family. Our daughter is a wanderer: she travels with a computer and as a graphic designer she works from any place in the world. Our granddaughter is a singer, travelling Australia with a band. We meet up in a house-sit together for four weeks. Family stuff done, we are away again, the road always calling. What's around the next corner? We haven't been down there, let's check it out... And so it has been for ten years.

For the last three years we have been retired; until then, I supplemented our income with a bit of part-time work around the country – driving buses, pouring petrol, picking grapes, apples, apricots, packing shelves, driving a tram. You don't need much to live on. We belong to the New Zealand Motorhome Association with 2,500 properties to stay at, many of them free and others a donation of a gold coin. Solar panels, diesel heater and gas cooking make us completely self-contained; if the sun hides and our batteries are getting down we have our generator. A Department of Conservation pass allows us to stay up to three weeks at each DOC camp before we have to move. Though I'm retired, there is always something to do.

As I write this we have stopped for the winter. I'm looking out of our van windows on our bit of land towards the Ruahine Ranges with snow on the tops. Grey misty clouds are starting to creep towards us, the wind is picking up; we feel close to nature. Will we go back to a house? Maybe one day we might buy a smaller van and build a very small cottage on our section. But for now we are content. While our health is with us, we will keep going. Our adventure has not stopped. There will be another day tomorrow and another road to drive.

Owen Clough, ex-New Zealand Air Force, former bus and tram driver, salesman and business owner, is from the earthquake city of Christchurch, New Zealand. Now retired, he used his hobby of genealogy and history to write his first novel, *Whispers of the Past*. He travels New Zealand in his motorhome with his wife, Kaye.

Charlie's Party Trick
Julia Hammond

'Are you sure this is such a good idea?'

It was hard not to slip on the track leading to what passed for a dock on the San Juan de Pequini River. The previous night had seen heavy rains, to be expected at this time of year, but the morning had dawned bright, the sky clear. Seeing the river running high and fast, however, hammered home the point that there were better seasons to be taking a trip upriver in a dugout canoe. The ever more persistent thumping of my heart was becoming harder to ignore.

The situation was surely worse for my travelling companion. Holidaying with his carer, Charlie was a cheery octogenarian who revealed a mouthful of perfectly even teeth with every broad grin. Since breaking a hip four years before, he'd been wheelchair-bound. As spirited as his mop of unruly white hair, he wasn't about to let those four wheels become his prison. He'd long held the desire to visit Panama and had badgered his carer, Elsa, until she agreed to accompany him.

Our boatman, Anselmo, his body more heavily tattooed than David Beckham's, called upon a couple of local youths to help lift Charlie in his wheelchair onto the canoe. As they lashed the wheelchair to wooden slats that had seen better days, the rest of us clambered aboard. We set off upstream. At first, all was calm, and policia birds, named for their black and yellow colouring, flitted between the reeds that grew in the shallows. Soon, however, the clear waters clouded with rich clay, rushing past the bow of the boat carrying broken tree branches and muck from the overnight storms. Alarmingly fast, branches became logs which churned the river into a swirling torrent. Though a dunking could prove catastrophic for him more than anyone, Charlie retained his composure, smiling serenely atop his high perch, a soothing influence for the rest of us.

The boat began to struggle. Hitting a log could capsize us and Anselmo wasn't about to take a chance with his precious cargo. He indicated that we were pulling over to wait for the water level to subside. We had no idea how long this would take and waited anxiously, roped to a tree with roots half-exposed on a heavily eroded bank. Midges nibbled at our ankles, dragging attention away from our watery plight. We attempted a picnic, but no-one had much of an appetite.

Eventually, Anselmo asked us whether we felt it was time to continue and we agreed, figuring that he wouldn't have asked if it wasn't safe.

Disembarking at Embera Puru village was a challenge, not least for the men who had to carry Charlie in his chair like sedan-bearers. The gravel bank that served as a landing stage was still under several feet of water and I was forced to grab at the long grass to heave myself up the slippery mud. I thought about asking Charlie if I could sit on his lap but then wondered what would happen if the cheeky man were to agree.

Everyone in the village had turned out to greet us, men in loincloths and women in brightly patterned cotton skirts. Charlie was wheeled into a hall used for communal gatherings where he attracted a crowd of kids. Meanwhile, the rest of us were invited to climb a ladder into the hut that served as a rudimentary kitchen. Some of the women were cooking spiced chicken and fried plantain under its thick thatched roof.

Children played ball in a clearing, sure-footed despite the slick ground. I noticed that the older villagers looked out for them; to an extent parenting and supervision was communal. Idly, my thoughts strayed to the past, reminded of days when kids enjoyed more freedom and needed fewer expensive toys to keep them happy. Lush rainforest cocooned the village and it was an idyllic scene.

But that idyll was a deception. We joined Charlie to listen to the village chief, elected for a four-year term, as he explained how life had changed for the Embera people. Originally from the Darién region of southern Panama, the villagers had lived in Chagres National Park for thirty years or so and the Panamanian government imposed restrictions on what they could do and how they could use the forest. Their way of life was under threat.

Turning to tourism was their lifeline, and they had escaped possible exploitation by tour operators by forming a cooperative to ensure that income was shared. I wandered around to peruse the crafts that were offered for sale: plant fibre masks coloured with natural plant dyes, watertight woven baskets and tiny carved tagua nuts.

Calling us to attention, it was announced that the villagers were about to perform traditional dances for us. All the women of the village, arranged in height order right down to the smallest child, paraded in a ring and stamped their feet to a traditional rhythm. As anywhere, the teenage boys laughed at the teenage girls, ribbing them as they took part and leaving them blushing. Some of the men played flutes, drums and other percussion instruments and we were encouraged to join in with the dancing. Charlie shouted encouragement as the rest of us made fools of ourselves to polite applause.

After the dancers had dispersed, a crowd of children gathered around Charlie in his wheelchair. Open-mouthed, the youngest whooped and squealed, running off laughing before hurrying back to his side. Why was Charlie so entertaining to those kids? Elsa rolled her eyes and grinned. From her reaction, it would seem that this wasn't the first time this had happened.

I didn't have to wonder for long. The old character, seeing that we were watching, repeated his party trick for us too, removing his false teeth to reveal a gummy grin.

Julia Hammond is a travel writer and blogger. You'll find her in Bradt's *Bus-Pass Britain Rides Again*. She's published a number of Unanchor guidebooks and she blogs regularly for a range of online publications. Her travels have taken her across the globe but she's happiest walking her dogs near her Essex home.

Midnight Sun
Malcolm Singer

I was already above the Arctic Circle when I took a bus from Rovaniemi, heading north. After two weeks hitchhiking up from Helsinki through Finland, today I would cross into the northernmost part of Norway. The bus dropped me at Lakselv on the coast, and I secured a bed in a hostel. Happily, hostels are no longer only for youth, but accommodate people of all ages, even people like me in their sixties. It was 10 p.m., but still light outside. I figured I would read for an hour and then try to get a normal night's sleep. It turned out to be anything but.

Instead of going to bed, the three German men sharing the dorm room with me were going out to view the midnight sun. They invited me to join them, and I squeezed into the back of their old VW bug. Lakselv sits at the bottom of a fjord that opens directly north. We drove out to the edge of the fjord and looked out at the sun sitting above the northern horizon, the mountains on either side. It was about 11 p.m. by then, and we settled in to watch. Bothersome mosquitoes droned around us, so we gathered wood and made a smoky fire to keep them away.

The sun moved from left to right, gradually dipping closer and closer to the horizon. It never got there. At exactly midnight, there it sat, a red disk, perfectly framed by the mountains to each side and horizon below. It was a profound moment, the most profound of all, even after my lifetime of travel. I felt privileged to be standing just there at precisely that moment. My senses were sharp, acutely aware of the beautiful and dramatic setting.

After midnight, having passed its low point above the horizon, the sun began to rise as it moved to the right. About 1 a.m. it passed behind a mountain. We settled down, too excited to think about leaving anytime soon. The sky above us filled with clouds, and it began to rain. The fire fizzled, and the mosquitoes descended upon us. We quickly scrounged around for more wood and relit the fire.

About 2 a.m. I stood and watched the sun rise above the other side of the mountain. But this was no ordinary sunrise: I knew the sun had never set at all. The instant the first speck of sun appeared I stared open-mouthed, aware of the moment. I looked at the growing speck of the sun, then down at my feet, then slowly up again, taking in the ground before me, the fjord, the mountains. I didn't just feel, I *knew* and understood the continuity of time and the connection between my body and all that was around me. I was simply and purely at one with the universe. It had taken me over six decades to reach that realisation.

For the remainder of that night rain came and went, and we kept feeding the fire. Around 4 a.m. it rained so hard there was no hope of restarting it. The mosquitoes came back, this time in force, and we got up and ran to escape them. There was a cloud of mosquitoes; they were everywhere. We got to a tree and found several square feet of dry moss, ripped it up and quickly made another fire. The moss burned intensely, and we had a brief respite, but within a couple of minutes it had burnt out and the mosquitoes attacked again. On we pushed, and in that moment of torment another truth came to me: I finally understood why ancient people continued to migrate southward through the Americas, not stopping until they reached the bottom of the continent at Tierra del Fuego. They were trying to get away from the damn mosquitoes! Every molecule of my body understood this fact and in our onward trek to escape the swarm, we became primitive, migrating man. As if through a blizzard, on we marched, heading for some place on earth where we could settle and be free from the torment pursuing us. We were leaving Africa. We were Neanderthals. We were Aborigines. When would our travails ever end?

The answer came with a jolt. A jet took off from Lakselv Airport and soared into the sky. We looked at it, instantly transported back to reality: we were backpackers, three young Germans and an aged American, wet and cold, and we needed to get back to the hostel. We ran to the VW, piled in, and drove off.

Born and raised in New York, **Malcolm Singer** taught physics and mathematics as a Peace Corps Volunteer in Ghana in the late 1960s. After returning, he taught at the United Nations International School and San Francisco University High School until retiring in 2009. He lives in Oakland, California.